THE CHRISTIAN AND HIS BIBLE

THE CHRISTIAN
AND HIS BIBLE

By
DOUGLAS JOHNSON

1953
WM. B. EERDMANS PUBLISHING COMPANY
GRAND RAPIDS, MICHIGAN

First Edition – September 1953

CONTENTS

PREFACE

THE Bible presents unique claims concerning its own nature and message. The experienced Christian will have little difficulty in conceding these claims. Today, however, there are many students and educated young people for whom this most important book ranks little more than one amongst a number of literary 'classics'. Several factors account for this undervaluation and consequent neglect. The writer is convinced, however, that by far the commonest reason for the current depreciations is ignorance, or misunderstanding, of what the Bible itself says, and what it does *not* say, concerning its own nature and purpose. It is chiefly to a consideration of these two subjects that the following pages will be directed.

Already there exist numerous and more scholarly books concerning the Bible. To add to them may appear unnecessary or, even, an impertinence. This venture has been made simply because experience suggests to the writer that along some such lines students may be induced again to take up the Bible and to study it with less prejudiced minds.

The writer makes no pretence to originality. He has made use of the experience of several friends whose knowledge and scholarship are vastly superior to his. Chief amongst these must be named D. Martyn Lloyd-Jones, M.D., M.R.C.P., N. B. Stonehouse, D.D., and D. J. Wiseman, M.A. None of these, however, must be held responsible for any errors or deficiencies which may still remain in the MS. The writer is aware that he resembles the threadbare spectator who had been 'at a great feast of languages and stolen the scraps.'

D. J.

THE VOICE OF GOD IN HIS CHURCH

WHETHER God still speaks in His Church is a question of the greatest importance to every Christian man and woman. Perhaps the simplest way to demonstrate and to illustrate its relevance will be to attempt to place ourselves in the position of a group of Christians at the close of the first century A.D. Avoiding as far as may be all unnecessary technicalities, let us attempt to reconstruct a situation which must repeatedly have been re-enacted in little Christian communities throughout the Near East, the Balkan Peninsula and, perhaps, North Africa. The occasion, which we shall describe in a single early Christian community, was fraught with possibility for good or ill throughout the whole of the infant Church.

The scene is set in a meeting place of the church in Thessalonica, one of the chief cities of Macedonia, in the year A.D. 103. The church has concluded its worship, and a Christian merchant has arrived from Ephesus. He has just shared the important news that John the apostle, who had been in exile and imprisonment for years on the island of Patmos, is reported to have died a year or two earlier. The matter is of vital moment because John the apostle was the last of the little group of disciples who had personally heard and talked with Jesus. So far as they know, the final direct link between their generation and Jesus of Nazareth, whom they have been taught to worship as Lord and Head of their church, has now been severed.

It more and more dawns upon them that the news is even more serious than might at first sight appear. It is true that their own church had been founded by another missionary, the apostle Paul, and that, characteristically, he had bequeathed to them a good deal of careful instruction before he had left their district. They also possess two 'apostolic' letters which had officially been addressed to them by their missionary founder. Also they themselves had not long since submitted by letter certain difficulties for John's advice. The churches in Asia had constantly consulted him in this way. By virtue of his seniority, and his apostleship, his opinions had hitherto been accepted as final. But now that he is no longer available, they are beginning to wonder who, in future, will fill for the various churches the same advisory rôle? As it happens, they themselves have recently been meeting several differences of opinion on important matters and have begun to think of sending a messenger with a letter about these debatable points to the aged apostle. It is quickly agreed that they must meet again the following evening to consider the new situation in which the church now finds itself. They are no longer in direct touch with any of those who had been appointed by the Lord Himself to the apostleship and to the leadership of the first churches.

The next evening, being assembled, the most senior of the elders prays for guidance and briefly outlines what it is they have met to discuss. He proposes that they shall explore together the channels through which they may expect God to guide them as a faithful Christian community. He emphasizes that it is of the greatest importance that they shall come to a common mind concerning what in future shall be their ultimate court of appeal in those matters where they are not agreed. As is customary under the gentle administration of this church, the members are invited to express their views in open session.

I. CENTRAL DISCIPLINE

The first to intervene is a former centurion of the Imperial Army. He speaks briskly and to the point. It all seems quite plain to *him*! Is it conceivable that God has left such an important matter to chance? No doubt it will be found that He had commanded the apostles duly to appoint their successors, and they will already have transferred to such their special authority and other apostolic powers. These men will continue to regulate the major affairs of the churches throughout their regions by virtue of their succession from the apostles. To the senior elder (a fisherman), however, the matter is not at all so obvious! In the first place, neither their own apostle, Paul, nor the senior apostle, John, had given them instructions about any such transference of their particular apostolic powers to others. Secondly, and on the contrary, Paul had spoken as if the *whole Church* was in 'the apostolic succession' and that the leaders were to be instituted for their special functions in each local church. He was for ever emphasizing the importance of the duties of the *local* elders. He had repeatedly asserted that, whilst remaining in as close and as cordial relations as they could with all other churches, they were to regard themselves in Thessalonica as possessing all that was needed of divine authority and guidance for the full discharge of their duties as a complete local expression of the 'Great Congregation of God'.

The centurion agrees that they are supposed to have all that they need by way of authority for *local* affairs in the form of their own body of elders and deacons. But he asks what will happen (as indeed has already begun to happen) when they do not agree upon the essentials? And, in any case, who will adjudicate when they disagree with, for example, their Christian visitors from the neighbouring churches in Berea or Philippi? Discipline is needed; at least, *that* is what his army experience has taught him! Discipline is what a region-wide church must have, and they can get it in the last analysis only by appointing one man in general authority for each main area. Several at this point ask what will happen when whole regions disagree. To the centurion the answer is obvious. For, at this point, a 'generalissimo' must be brought in who can give a final ruling which none will dare to question!

To a tutor in a wealthy family the centurion's reasoning appears to be unsupported by the evidence, and even dangerous. He points out that, even if army methods were necessarily right, none of the apostles has led them to expect any such arrangement to be transferred into the churches. In any case, they had not been told the name of Paul's designated successor, and no one, it now seems, knows who was appointed to succeed John! One member asks whether it might not be Timothy? For Paul had sometimes seemed to treat his companion as if he expected him to succeed. But here, again, another member of the little church reminds them that Timothy himself had been quite emphatic, when several members of the church at Philippi had visited

Ephesus, that he could 'never be another Paul'. It was Timothy, too, who—when he had helped to ordain elders in a new church in the region of Ephesus—had declared that the most he could do was to share his experience of Paul's teaching and methods if they cared to consult him. The senior elder at this point interrupts to say that it has for some months been in his mind to suggest that they should cease to look to distant 'authorities' to make rulings for them in difficult matters. The fact is that there is now left no single living person who actually saw and was intimate with the Lord Jesus. The time has now come to ask God to show them how any given local church, particularly those remote from the help of experienced leaders, can hear God's voice finally speaking upon any given matter of faith or conduct. He suggests that they may have been neglecting something which they have been told.

II. GOD-GIVEN REASON OR COMMON SENSE

At this point the tutor intervenes to suggest that it seems to him that they do not value sufficiently the intellects which God has given them! They have minds and, surely, God expects them to be used. The more he has studied Plato and Aristotle the more he is amazed to find how far those pagan philosophers were able to travel towards the truth, simply by using their own minds. In fact, when one of Paul's letters had recently been read to them, he had noticed several phrases which were reminiscent of Plato! He goes on to suggest that if God has given men minds, and especially if these minds have been redeemed, then *reason* is 'obviously' destined to be the ultimate authority in the Church. In any case, the 'redeemed mind' offers the possibility of a unity which will solve all their problems. He suggests that all they need to do is to apply themselves to the 'Holy Writings', to cull from them what obviously still makes sense, and then to welcome all that their enlightened minds approve from whatsoever source it comes!

At this, however, a freed slave ventures to speak. He confesses that he is only a working man and that he often cannot follow all that is debated in some of their discussions. But what has just been said does not sound right to him. Not long after he had become a Christian, Paul the apostle, who was then in the city, had come out to the quarries where he was working and had given him a hand with his task. He will always remember that day as long as he lives! The apostle had a way of always making him understand every word. Paul had clearly explained to him that although the Christian has been redeemed to God, yet his mind and body were still to be regarded as only the 'tools' or instruments through which His Spirit works. In themselves they were to be regarded as neither good nor bad. They could be put either to a good, or to a bad use. The important thing for the Christian, or for that matter a whole church, was to be sure that he went to the right place to hear the voice of the Good Shepherd and to take care not to be misled by 'the voice of strangers'. The apostle had advised him not to worry about his being unable to understand the complicated arguments of the educated men, because they usually made more difficulties than they ever solved. He remembers quite distinctly that the apostle had warned him not to be taken in by some who were tending to mix up the ideas of heathen philosophers, such as Plato and Aristotle, with the revelation which God had given by His Spirit. The apostle had also said (and he had noticed that it came also in the last part of Paul's letter to the church in Rome when a copy was read out in their church) that their minds had need to be cleansed and readjusted so that they would cease to think like the pagans around them. They needed continually to 'renew' their thought-life so that they would come to have the mind of Christ their Saviour.

The senior elder commends him for this suggestion and adds that he is sure that this point is important. His recollection of what Paul the apostle had taught them is much the same. He agrees, of course, that God expects them to use their minds. But Paul had urged continually that they must bring 'every thought into captivity to the obedience of Christ'. Human reason is not enough. In itself it is an equivocal and may even be a deceitful guide.

III. GOD-GIVEN INTUITION

The women members of the church now begin to ask how they are to know the mind of Christ. It is not so easy for them to work along some of the lines proposed by the men and by the same methods to know what they ought to do. They ask if God does not ordinarily use the natural gifts He has given. So far as they are concerned, they suggest that He may intend to make them more sensitive to inward impressions and to heighten their powers of intuition. Indeed, they ask whether His Holy Spirit has not been sent to bring about just *that*! In other words, in the same way that the Holy Spirit is received by an individual and He causes her natural 'feelings' to be more sensitive towards God, so in the church ought they not to expect to achieve an intuitive 'group mind' concerning this or that? Guided by the Holy Spirit they might even expect regularly to become unanimous on any given point. The senior elder points out that though it is a good ideal to work for unanimity in any company, yet experience suggests that it is not always very easy, particularly as personalities and 'vested interests' so often insinuate themselves into the problem. It is pointed out also that if strong intuitions were relied upon some would tend to feel passionately on both sides of a dispute. It is usually these same strong feelings, and sometimes prejudice, which make it so difficult for many to listen to arguments put forward by the other side. Also, if they give free rein to their inward feelings, there will be a danger of having almost as many views as there are people.

IV. THE VOICE OF THE SPIRIT

Another member suggests, however, that this is leaving out of account the Holy Spirit. Can they not trust Him to secure the unity they want by controlling their intuitions and feelings? In reply it is pointed out that, whilst they would not wish for one moment to under estimate the functions of the Holy Spirit, yet Paul the apostle had always been very emphatic on this particular point. He had explained how that, whilst the Holy Spirit might at times make use of their intuitions, yet it would never do for the whole of a community to look to intuition as its ultimate authority! He had illustrated how necessary it is for all to look to an external standard or point of reference (such as, for example, Israel had possessed in the divine law) above the inexplicable and unpredictable impulses which control our thoughts and actions.

He had pointed out that there lurks here a special danger because it is all too easy to identify one's own feelings with the voice of the Holy Spirit. The apostle had also been most insistent that the Spirit's voice was usually to be heard speaking only in and through the Holy Scriptures. The doctrine of 'the inner light' needed to be treated with some care!

V. CONSCIENCE

At this point, one of the younger elders asks if they have not been overlooking the authority of conscience. The apostle Peter, whom he had heard on one of his journeys to Palestine, had given an impressive sermon on keeping the faith with 'a pure conscience'. Is this not the final arbiter for which they have been looking? If they all can act strictly according to their conscience, how could they—the Holy Spirit helping them—possibly go wrong? Yet, once again, there are those to remind him that they will not necessarily reach finality that way! Quite recently they have been taunted by their pagan neighbours because the conscience of the centurion has allowed him to be a successful recruiting-sergeant for the Imperial Forces, whilst in Berea, two young men have been martyred because, on grounds of conscience, they had refused to bear arms.

VI. THE HOLY SCRIPTURES

They do not seem to be getting anywhere. At last, however, the slave and quarry-worker ventures to ask if he can tell further of Paul the apostle's conversation when they had walked back from the quarries. The veteran missionary had explained how he, a poor working-man, who could not even read, might know more about God and about His will than many of the rich, the university men and the philosophers. He had demonstrated how a whole church, as well as an individual, could come to know the will of God in any given matter. Paul took his illustrations from ordinary life. The apostle had said something like this: 'If you want to know what a person is like or what he thinks, then you must pay great attention not only to what he does, but to his actual words. Second-hand reports are often misleading. You must see the man himself and hear what he himself has to say. It is his *words* and deeds which matter more than anything else.

Listen carefully to the readings from "the Holy Writings" and if possible learn them by heart.' He kept repeating, 'Listen carefully to the readings; pay great attention to the words of the Holy Writings!'

VII. THE WORD AND THE SPIRIT

He is asked by the tutor what he thought of some of the points of the Bible which are not, as they stand, easily to be understood. Also, what are they to do when confronted by new experiences and new problems about which the apostles have not taught them? The slave replies: 'Yes, that is the other lesson which Paul the apostle gave me. He said, "God has not only given to His Church the Holy Writings, but He has also given His Holy Spirit to dwell in the hearts of believers and to be in the whole Church the official Interpreter of what is written. The Holy Spirit is also the Guide who will help us singly or together, to apply the controlling principles revealed in the Holy Writings to any given case as it may arise." It was at this point that the apostle helped me so much, because he illustrated how I could be guided in all the little problems of my own life which are not mentioned in the actual Writings. He said it would mean constant practice and that it would come only to those who were prepared humbly to "walk by faith."

This statement meets with the complete approval of several of the older men present. All that this wise slave has said is entirely in keeping with what Paul the apostle had said to them, especially when he finally took leave of their company in Thessalonica. He had reiterated again and again to the elders who had walked some distance from the city with him: 'For your final authority in all matters of faith and conduct you must always go to God speaking in and through the Holy Writings. Pay careful attention to their words. Do not meddle with them to suit your own wishes. In them you have the living and abiding speech of the Spirit of God.'

VIII. THE MIND OF CHRIST

Here we must leave the church in Thessalonica. In the above notes are no doubt several small anachronisms in the thinking which is attributed to its members. But we suggest that they were facing just such problems as have been described, though some of these may have been only in embryo. There have been outlined above some of the main points of the age-long discussions concerning the nature of God's instrument for ruling His Church. In the previous three paragraphs are stated the views which have provided the spiritual anchorage for those faithful Christians who have most closely adhered to the teaching of the apostles. It is the contention of this book that the New Testament plainly states that the voice of God to His people, whether collectively or singly, can be certainly heard only by accepting the words of the Holy Spirit speaking in and through the Holy Scriptures. The following is one classic passage in the New Testament where Paul states his teaching as follows: 'But as it is written, Things which eye saw not, and ear heard not, And which entered not into the heart of man, Whatsoever things God prepared for them that love him. But unto us God revealed them through the Spirit: for the Spirit searcheth all things, yea, the deep things of God. For who among men knoweth the things of a man, save the spirit of the man, which is in him? even so the things of God none knoweth, save the Spirit of God. But we received, not the spirit of the world, but the spirit which is of God; that we might know the things that are freely given to us by God. Which things also we speak, not in words[1] which man's wisdom teacheth, but which the Spirit teacheth; comparing spiritual things with spiritual. Now the natural man receiveth not the things of the Spirit of God: for they are foolishness unto him; and he cannot know them, because they are spiritually judged. But he that is spiritual judgeth all things, and he himself is judged of no man. For who hath known the mind of the Lord, that he should instruct him? But we have the mind of Christ' (1 Cor. ii. 9–16).[2]

[1] In the first instance this reference might be to the oral rather than the written teaching of the apostles.

[2] Quotations in this book from the Bible are from the Revised Version (1881) unless otherwise stated.

CHAPTER TWO

THE BIBLE IN ITS PRESENT SETTING

(N.B.—It is suggested that the reader who is not interested in the commonest philosophical and general objections to the Christian's view of the Bible should pass over this and possibly the third chapter, beginning to read again at page 40.)

A FIRST necessity in the examination of any ancient manuscript is that the observer should be willing to allow the document to speak for itself. Ordinary justice—apart from strict scholarship—demands that all the internal evidence should first be carefully considered before information from external sources is borrowed, whether this be to serve as a corrective or in order to complete the picture. What follows in later chapters emerges from the conviction that it has been the widespread neglect of this elementary rule, when approaching the sacred writings of the Christian Church, which chiefly has brought upon recent generations their great spiritual loss. This is no small matter. For the place which the Bible will occupy amongst us is controlled by such considerations. First, as has already been suggested, it will depend primarily upon the Bible's own claims.[1] Second, it will also depend upon whether there are confirmatory evidences of the truth of its claims and, third, whether we are reasonably confident that we now possess accurate copies of the earliest manuscripts and whether they preserve for us the original meaning of the writers. The most important factor remains, of course, the internal evidence. As Samuel Butler has put it: 'The

---

[1] If the reader is still unfamiliar with the details of the birth, life, death and resurrection of our Lord Jesus Christ and the Bible's explanation of their true meaning, it is suggested that he should cover this gap in his knowledge and return to the present book at a later stage. He might commence with St. Luke's Gospel, followed by the Gospel of St. John, and then read how St. Paul applies the facts in his Epistle to the Romans. To obtain the right perspective it will be found best quietly to read St. John's Gospel at a single sitting.

only question concerning the authority of Scripture is whether it be what it claims to be—not whether it be a book of such sort, or so promulgated, as weak men are apt to fancy a book containing a divine revelation should (be).'

I. THE OLDER OBJECTIVISM AND MODERN SUBJECTIVISM

There is today a wide disparity between the almost unanimous voice of the great teachers and leaders throughout the first nineteen hundred years of Church history and the attitude of many scholars in our own time. The traditional 'Church' doctrine of Holy Scripture presents it as the book of which God is the primary author, and as one which possesses in itself such *objective* authority that loyal Christians are called upon to regard themselves as bound by its teaching. For example, a mediaeval writer puts the matter in this form: 'What is not contained in the Scriptures, or cannot with necessary and obvious consistency be deduced from the contents of the same, no Christian needs to believe' (Occam: *Dialogues*). Similarly, amongst the Continental Reformers, Luther when under duress states his refusal to recant in the following historic words: 'I am conquered by the Writings (i.e. passages of Scripture) cited by me, and my conscience is captive to the Word of God.' In his 'De Ordine' Luther declares: 'God's Word stands incomparably high above the Church; in this Word she, as a creature, cannot resolve, order, or execute but can only be resolved, ordered and carried out. For who generates his father? who has first called his Creator into being?'

By contrast, widespread views are today advanced of quite another kind. Variously expressed and variously applied, the ultimate result will most often be found to be a lowered view of Scripture. The change has come about through nearly one hundred years of (i) the most rigorous linguistic and historical criticism of the documents as they have come down to us, (ii) the rise of a philosophy of science which is based upon purely agnostic, or atheistic, assumptions, and (iii) a movement on a world-wide scale away from religion as a whole. In the result, the Bible has for large numbers of people been quietly relegated to the possession of little more than *subjective* authority. That is, it has come to be assumed that its own statements must now be received only with certain modifications, depending upon the view of the observer. It may be conceded that it retains a commanding influence over those who happen to be attracted by it and so choose to have it so. But, for the rest who are not particularly interested, it may simply be treated as another of the world's greatest books. Such an attitude has been expressed at its clearest in Coleridge's well-known words of the Bible's useful-ness in so far as he was concerned: 'I have found words for my inmost thoughts, songs for my joy, utterances for my hidden griefs, and pleadings for my shame. In short, *whatever finds me, bears witness for itself that it has proceeded from a Holy Spirit.*' But, we may ask, what of those parts of the Bible which, at any given time, he did not seem to need and which in certain moods did not 'find' him? Are they less the product of 'a Holy Spirit'?

We shall do well, then, to give careful attention to what the Bible itself declares concerning its authority. In later chapters will be considered the impact of modern scholarship, the growth of the natural sciences, and those other developments which have obscured the true nature and value of the Bible.

II. DO CHRISTIANS REASON IN A CIRCLE?

Several further preliminary considerations, however, must here be noticed. The question may arise in the mind of a reader who is philosophically inclined: 'Is there not a danger of reasoning in a circle? Are you not allowing the Bible to be judge in its own cause?' Such an objection is, of course, constantly urged by non-Christians against the Christian gospel as a whole. Thought-ful people who are attracted by the Bible's message and who assert that they would like to act upon it if only they could be satisfied that it were *really true*, attribute their indecision to just such a difficulty. They would put their problem to us in this way: 'What Christians seem to us to say is something like this: "God has stated in the Bible that He is true; therefore He is true." In other words, you Christians start with the assumption of the reliability of the Bible and you then proceed to require us to accept all that the Book itself says concerning the existence of God, the teaching of Christ, God's requirements of mankind and so on. Or, you just simply assert that *God has declared* the

Bible to be true and that is supposed to conclude the argument! We suggest that what you are really offering is an attempt to prove God's truth by the truth of God.' In other words, the difficulty that many feel is that the Christian's whole system of thought is a vast 'petitio principii' because it assumes at the outset (i) that God exists, (ii) that He is true, (iii) that He is willing to make Himself known to us and (iv) that in the Bible we have a record of what He has thus been pleased to make known.

The truest—and perhaps the wisest—answer that the Christian may return is to acknowledge that so far as formal logic is concerned this is exactly what he seems to be doing. In the nature of the case, it is all he can do if he is to free himself from all the other diverse forms of circular reasoning which are displayed by the philosopher and the scientist! All mankind argues alike in a circle because (even with the help of mathematical abstractions which in the last analysis are irrational and sometimes border on the ridiculous) the human mind is never quite able to escape such elements of reasoning whenever it attempts an approach to an ultimate explanation of the universe. The philosopher (and, even more, the scientist) has not yet been born who is able to give a final explanation of his 'system', which is entirely free from arbitrary assumption and an element of 'the circle'. Illustrations could easily be multiplied. It is commonest, however, for those who today desire to explain the world apart from any 'introduction of a personal God' to commence their task by explaining that they are at the outset excluding the 'God-concept' and intend to utilize only what they call historical or scientific 'facts'. In other words, their initial assumption is that 'there is no God' and then they go on to complete their small circular system without any introduction of such a God. It may fairly be commented that they do at least succeed in bringing things 'down to earth'! Having, however, deliberately excluded all that can be considered 'supernatural', they then find themselves hard put to it to give satisfying explanations of even the simplest forms of truth, beauty and goodness—to say nothing of the categories which are usually found among the 'spiritual' attainments of mankind.

The writer is, of course, aware that just because everyone else argues in a circle, this fact does not justify the Christian in so doing, nor can it in any way assist to authenticate his own case. The consequence is the purely negative one that it ill becomes those who reject the Christian position to do so purely on such grounds, unless indeed they are prepared for consistent agnosticism and a final pessimism in the realm of thought. The fact is that several generations of Christians have tended to allow themselves to be overawed by arguments and attacks from non-Christians which do not withstand a robust counter-scrutiny.

The reader will find it a wholesome mental exercise to notice carefully the starting points and ruthlessly to examine the concepts which are regarded as 'axiomatic' in the writings of philosophers and scientists. The Christian, at least, has every reason for reminding some of those who 'do protest too much' of the homely proverb: 'People living in glass houses should learn not to throw stones!' The fact is that all philosophies are founded upon a basic *pre-scientific choice* which is in the last analysis adherence to some non-rational, fundamental idea, which comes far more within the sphere of 'religion' than those of philosophy or natural science.

III. GOD'S INITIATIVE AND THE NATURE OF TRUTH

The Christian, granted his original premiss, sees clearly that this must necessarily be so. For if both God and also man be at all as the Bible itself describes them, then the only possible revealer of God must be *God Himself*. God throughout must take the initiative, and He alone can demonstrate to man the true nature of the Godhead. He alone can provide a self-revelation in such words as will convey any adequate and suitable impressions to minds which are so vastly inferior and also different in kind. It is God alone who can break into the little circle of human knowledge. In the nature of the case how He does it and what He says will be 'sui generis'.

In other words, there is bound up with final truth a basic self-authenticating quality. When approached in humility it is something which compels conviction. The corresponding human reaction must be one of faith and acceptance, with all its implications. 'Faith'—of a kind—is surely a pre-requisite in other departments of human knowledge, though in this case the term is used with a lowered meaning. The word in a Christian context carries a special and exclusive reference. The essential message of the Christian religion comes to a man in a compelling personal form. It is the truth embodied in Christ. He is the supreme revelation of God and must be accepted or rejected on His own merits. If the Bible statements concerning God, man, and the nature of human sin be true at all, then man can expect no knowledge of God other than through God's own initiative and His own witness to Himself. If that be so, then the only possible and proper reaction on the human side is full, free, submissive and confiding faith—the due response of the creature to Creator, of the finite to the Infinite, and of the rebel to the condescending, yet always Sovereign, Lord. With Anselm, he who would find the truth of God must acknowledge: *Credo ut intelligam* ('I believe in order that I may understand').

IV. THE MAJOR PROBLEM

It is at this point imperative to emphasize what is often overlooked in discussions of this matter. The Bible itself constantly asserts and illustrates the fact that, in revealing Himself to man, God was confronted with what, humanly speaking, were two great difficulties. The first was man's limited intelligence. The finite creature cannot comprehend the infinite Creator. But the second was far more significant and serious. Man, who desperately needed the revelation, was living in a state of sin and rebellion. There was a *moral* obstruction to the understanding of the true nature of the one true and holy God. The Bible expressly states that it was on account of this second factor that the wisdom and love of God chose to overcome it and to reveal the Godhead in the form of a Person. The major purpose of the coming of this Person was to perform a great redeeming and reconciling act. The Bible states that Jesus Christ did not come simply to provide a *personal* revelation of God His Father and to give (what is in fact) the world's most beautiful doctrinal and ethical teaching. He came primarily to be the Redeemer and Reconciler. Before he can begin to appreciate the nature of God, man requires not simply intellectual enlightenment; his primary needs are repentance, faith in Christ, forgiveness and reconciliation. Hence, the central point of God's revelation to man must always be located in the life, death and resurrection of Christ. As 'the Mediator between God and man' He performed the double task of revealing and redeeming. In biblical thinking, the incarnation, the death and resurrection of Christ are all one great intervention by God. Here come together the two principles of revelation and redemption which remain throughout the Bible closely intertwined.

The most important considerations have seldom been put more succinctly or forcefully than by Calvin, the sixteenth-century reformer, in his *Institutes of the Christian Religion*: 'How can the human mind, by its own efforts, penetrate into an examination of the essence of God, when it is totally ignorant of its own. Wherefore, let us freely leave to God the knowledge of Himself. For "He alone," as Hilary says, "is a competent witness to Himself, being only known by Himself" ' (*Inst.* I. xiii. 21). 'Although man had remained immaculately innocent this condition would have been too mean for him to approach to God without a Mediator' (*Inst.* II. xii. 1). 'Since the whole Bible proclaims that He was clothed in flesh in order to become a Redeemer, it argues excessive temerity to imagine another cause or another end for it. The end for which Christ was promised from the beginning is sufficiently known: it was to restore a fallen world and to succour ruined men' (*Inst.* II. xii. 4). In speaking of our position today Calvin adds: 'God alone is a sufficient witness concerning Himself, and He does not manifest Himself to men otherwise than through the Word' (*Commentary*, Gn. iii. 6). 'This, then, must be considered as a fixed principle, that in order to enjoy the light of true religion, we ought to begin with teaching from heaven; and that no man can have the least taste of pure and wholesome teaching, save him who will be a disciple of Scripture' (*Inst.* I. vi. 2).

V. A PARALLEL FROM OUR LORD'S TIME

Arguments against the self-authenticating witness of the Bible are by no means new. Our Lord Himself was criticized on exactly these grounds by the Pharisees of His day. He did not, however, regard the criticism very seriously. The case is stated in the Gospel records as follows: 'The Pharisees therefore said unto him, "Thou bearest witness of thyself; thy witness is not true." Jesus answered and said unto them, "Though I bear witness of myself, yet my witness is true: for I know whence I came, and whither I go." ' Our Lord then went on to explain that they were judging purely by human standards and had forgotten the criteria of the 'supernatural'. He pointed out that even according to their own law *two* witnesses were required in such a matter. He then declared that the One that sent Him (i.e. His divine Father) is the first Witness, and He is the second Witness. Since, however, they did not know God, His Father, they had also failed to recognize Him as God the Son.

The position of the Bible today presents a somewhat close parallel—which, however, must not be pressed in detail. Those who do not recognize the Bible for what it claims to be—i.e. the self-authenticating Word of God—are quick to say: 'But it witnesses to itself and so its witness is not valid'. The Bible's reply is that the modern man, by ruling out in advance all idea of the supernatural world, has failed to recognize both the witness of the Bible and also that of the other chief Witness. God Himself speaks to the world in and through the Bible which they are responsible to accept and to obey.

Indeed, the explanations of the New Testament in all this matter emphasize that one of the characteristics of sinful men has been that 'they did not like to retain God in their knowledge', and this has inevitably led to various limiting and evil consequences which they suffer. On its side the Bible calls upon men to hear the Holy Spirit, as God's witness, speaking in their own consciences and through the pages of Holy Scripture, concerning all those matters which the unenlightened and unaided human mind can never know. For, once again, it is abundantly evident that if we once grant that God is Someone whose life and thought transcends that of all humanity, then the only One who can give a true and satisfying answer concerning all that is beyond the limits of our own little world of space and time is *God Himself*. To talk of true 'religion without revelation' will be nonsense.

Equally important, it will be impossible for the unaided human reason to offer more than so-called 'proofs' (or, more accurately, confirmations) to underline and to illustrate that which has already been received only through the faith which God Himself imparts to the humble and penitent seeker. The very idea of a revelation from God requires that the *initiative* shall come entirely from the other side of the great divide. It must be a movement from the unlimited God towards a very limited mankind. We are, therefore, compelled to start all our reasoning just where the Bible itself starts, that is with the categorical assertion of a temporal creation, viz. 'In the beginning, God created the heavens and the earth . . .'

VI. A UNIQUE HISTORICAL EVENT

Discussing the problem of authority in quite another setting and from a somewhat different angle, the philosopher, Professor A. E. Taylor, suggests that a valid argument cannot be made out for granting to the Bible the *objective* authority which it traditionally has held in the Church, because of the *subjective* element which is necessitated both (i) by the presence of the human writers in the production of the book, and also because of the contingencies of the historical incidents recorded, and (ii) the subjectivity which inevitably creeps in through the modern reader's interpretation and appreciation of what has been written. Yet he goes on to say, 'A theology which finds mystery it cannot explain away at the centre of things may not be true, but it is certain that a theology which professes to have cleared away all mystery out of the world must be false. In any true account of the concrete and individual reality one must somewhere come upon something of which it can only be said, "Why this thing should be so, or even just what it is, is more than I can tell, but at all costs it must be recognized that here the thing is." If this is all we mean by "irrationality" we may safely say that historical individuality is the great supreme irrational from which thought can never succeed in getting free' (*The Faith of a Moralist*, II. p. 212).

The Christian believes that in the case both of the bringing together of divinity and humanity in our Lord's Person when

He was born into this world, and also of the unique combination of the divine and human in Holy Scripture, we have two just such historical phenomena. The Bible itself has explained why God now deals 'mediately' (that is, indirectly) with mankind. It is man's sin which has alienated him from God. The Christian therefore declines to concede that, because man is now unable to deal with God directly and because the *Mediator* now speaks through Holy Scripture, these facts in any way lessen the objective authority of God's speech. God remains absolute and free to act or to speak just as He will. But the Bible states that it was the intrusion of human sin into the world that has caused God to withdraw Himself. It has been on grounds of reaction against sin and not of metaphysical necessity that God has put a distance between Himself and sinful man so that the prophet needs to lament, 'Verily thou art a God that hidest thyself' and 'Your sins have separated between you and your God, and your sins have hid his face from you, that he will not hear.'

VII. THE CHRISTIAN DISCLAIMS REASONING IN A CIRCLE

It may be well to make clear at this point that the Christian also disclaims the notion that he is *really* engaged in reasoning in a circle. He would, on the contrary, contend that what may seem to be no more than a piece of mundane circular reasoning, is totally transformed by a single concrete fact. It is of importance that this fact is presented as such in the evidence with which we are confronted in the New Testament itself. Challenged to show how the Bible's explanation of life, and of the universe in general, transcends any other which has been produced by poetic imagination or philosophic speculation, the Christian would unhesitatingly point to the resurrection of Christ. Here is the watershed of the New Testament. Once grant that the apostles were truthful, unmistaken and meticulous witnesses, and that we have an accurate report of their evidence, then the Christian regards his case as complete. There is much more to be said for granting this premiss than is ordinarily allowed by those who assail the Christian position. On enquiry, it is uncommon to find amongst such opponents those who have seriously examined the real grounds on which the Christian accepts the New Testament books as valid documents. Not only so, but it is almost equally rare to find amongst them more than a handful who have sought to make themselves accurately acquainted with the contents of these books. The author, therefore, makes no apology for urging again upon the reader the duty of familiarizing himself with what the apostles actually claimed for themselves and their message.[1]

VIII. THE CENTRAL CLAIM OF THE APOSTLES

The apostles are unanimous in their assertions that Jesus of Nazareth with whom they had lived for some three years was in fact the Son of God, and the long-promised Saviour King of Israel. They affirm that they are eyewitnesses of His resurrection (which He had foretold); that they have received His post-resurrection authentication of the Old Testament; that He has given His Holy Spirit to be the Guide and Ruler in His Church; and that they were present at, and saw, His ascent into heaven. They do not present the teaching of the Bible as a compilation which, conceivably, might have been simply the product of religious genius or poetic imagination. The Bible is not suspended, as it were, in mid-air. It is firmly anchored to historic happenings at stated points in space and time. The implications are drawn for us in unmistakable terms in the New Testament itself. To those who accept the apostolic witness as valid and who, with repentance and humility, receive Jesus Christ as Saviour, Lord and God, is given forgiveness and reconciliation with God. To know God is also to receive the illumination of the Holy Spirit and eternal life. Conversely, those who reject the apostolic witness imprison themselves within ordinary natural human reasoning, resist the divine initiative in revelation and redemption, and bring upon themselves final rejection and eternal loss. In the words of the apostle Peter in the New Testament: 'But Peter, standing . . . spake . . . saying . . . Jesus of Nazareth, a man approved of God unto you by mighty works and wonders and signs, which God did by him in the midst of you, even as ye yourselves know; him, being delivered up by the determinate counsel and foreknowledge of God, ye by the hand of lawless

[1] Read, for example, 1 Cor. i, ii and xv.

men did crucify and slay: . . . This Jesus did God raise up, whereof we all are witnesses. Being therefore by the right hand of God exalted, and having received of the Father the promise of the Holy Ghost, he hath poured forth this, which ye see and hear' (Acts ii. 14, 22, 23, 32, 33; see also 1 Cor. xv. 1-28).

In concluding this chapter, let us again emphasize that in the coming of the Son of God into the world to reveal God and to redeem man we have just such a single unusual happening of the kind concerning which the philosopher suggests that we exclaim: 'Why this thing should be so, or even just what it is, is more than I can tell, but . . . *here* the thing is.' The full story of this outstanding event and all that it means has been enshrined in a *unique* record. This record carries with it divine authority. Let us therefore reflect with humility upon the implications of those very characteristics of God's revelation in the Bible which have been most criticized. As Pascal so well reminds us in his 'Pensées': 'Had it been His will to overcome the stubbornness of the most hardened, He could have rendered them unable to doubt the truth of His essence, in revealing Himself manifestly to them as He will appear at the last day, amid thunderings and lightnings. . . . Not *thus* willed He to appear in His gentle advent; because so many men make themselves unworthy of His mercy, He willed to leave them deprived of the good which they refuse. It had not then been just that He should appear in a manner plainly divine and wholly capable of convincing men, but neither had it been just that He should come in so hidden a manner as not to be recognized by those who sincerely sought Him. He has willed to reveal Himself wholly to these, and thus (willing to appear openly to those who seek Him with their whole heart, and to hide Himself from those who fly Him with all their heart) He has so tempered the knowledge of Himself as to give signs of Himself visible to those who seek Him and obscure to those who seek Him not.

'There is enough light for those who wish earnestly to see and enough obscurity for those of a contrary mind. Therefore let men recognize the truth of religion in the very obscurity of religion, in the little light we have of it and in our indifference to the knowledge of it.'

CHAPTER THREE

GOD'S SELF-REVELATION[1]

IN its opening words the Bible, without further explanation or apology, confronts us with a God who is absolute. This all-powerful God is said to have designed and brought into being all celestial objects, including the world and the living things within it. There is no hint throughout the whole range of the sixty-six books which follow that this divine supremacy can ever be successfully challenged. On the contrary, the entire teaching of the Bible repeatedly emphasizes and illustrates that any attempt to thwart 'the most High' has consistently met with ignominious failure. The last book in the Bible lifts the un-challengeable power of God to a place of unimaginable grandeur. It for ever dismisses further possibility of any such revolt.

A question is at once prompted: 'If God is so essentially different and greater than ourselves how can we know anything worthwhile about Him and how can we be sure that He is interested at all in the destinies of the men whom He has made?' This haunting doubt becomes all the more insistent when our attention is arrested in the third chapter of the very first book of the Bible by the fact that mankind soon misused his relative freedom and authority and set out upon what has proved a long course of disastrous opposition. A second question soon emerges from the first: 'Even if the sovereign God has some pleasure in man in his first state of innocence, can He retain any interest for His creature in the latter's new state of rebellion and self-centredness?' A third question immediately follows: 'Granted that God may still to some extent be interested in man, yet since the Bible presents Him as so infinitely greater than ourselves, how can man begin to understand Him or attain any true idea of His requirements? And, even if man could begin to understand, how can he be reconciled to God and really learn to obey Him?'

[1] See the introductory note to chapter II, page 18.

The greater part of the Bible is addressed to the answer of these questions. It is affirmed that instead of discarding mankind —as He would have had every justification for doing—God graciously condescended to make a self-disclosure or (to use the customary theological term) to make a 'revelation' of Himself. The important point to notice is that it is God who first acts in planning and doing. This is the outstanding characteristic of the religion of the Bible. In it everything ultimately depends supremely upon the initiative, the self-disclosure and the redemptive acts performed by the very God who is being sought, worshipped and served by man.

I. IN WHAT FORM DOES GOD REVEAL HIMSELF?

The Bible describes God as revealing Himself in two main ways. First, He has in general dealt with man as a person who is capable of some degree of thought and action. The fact of His 'Godhead' and His creatorial power has been made known in the phenomena of the world of creation and in the course of history. This is in theological discussion usually termed 'general', or 'natural', revelation.

The Bible's references to such a revelation will be found in such sections as Ps. xix. 1–9 and Rom. i. 18–23. This general revelation is stated to be sufficient to impress upon man the power of God as Creator and Governor of the universe. St. Paul describes it in such a way as to suggest that it is sufficient to leave men without excuse. They are expected to make use of it, to bestir themselves and to seek God's special revelation (Rom. i. 20). This general revelation operates universally.

The second form of God's self-revelation may be called 'special', 'supernatural' or 'redemptive'. It involves an activity of God which is more than 'natural' in the course of world affairs. It is addressed specifically to man as being a sinner who needs redemption and it is understood only by those in whom a desire has been awakened to seek after God. Scripture constantly emphasizes that 'The secret of the Lord is with them that fear him' (Ps. xxv. 14), and 'If ye then, being evil, know how to give good gifts unto your children, how much more shall your heavenly Father give the Holy Spirit to them that ask him?' (Lk. xi. 13).

It is clear from the Bible that general revelation is chiefly concerned with God as the Creator—and valuable as it is in its own sphere, it is insufficient by itself to bring sinning man back to a state of reconciliation and full relationship with God the Redeemer. On the other hand, special revelation kept in isolation (dealing as it does with God as the Redeemer) is not appreciated by man in its full wonder or in its true proportion. It must be set against the background of the God in whose hand all things are created, sustained and controlled. It is not, however, the case that the two revelations are simply co-ordinate or complementary. The Bible most clearly states that God has revealed Himself as Creator and that this can be seen in the works of His hand. It is emphatic that man has no excuse for turning aside to idolatry or atheism. The Bible also clearly states that God has intervened in human history and that He has completed a great work of redemption of which the fruits are still being gathered to His glory and the good of mankind. Each revelation becomes then the more remarkable when seen in the full light of the other. We may well ask why so great a God should stoop at all to redeem rebellious man; and, in saving him, we see how really great is His act of redemption!

II. PROGRESSIVE SELF-REVELATION

The Old Testament describes for us several stages through which this redemptive revelation of God has been worked out. First, He selected a single person, Abraham, and then a whole nation, Israel, through whom all mankind might be given His special blessing. From the midst of Israel God chose a single tribe (Judah) and, then, a single family (that of Jesse) from which should come the royal line of the kingly Messiah, i.e. through David the son of Jesse. The story of God's progressive self-revelation is worked out in a series of appearances to specially chosen individual patriarchs and later through historical acts in the national history of Israel. Finally comes a long line of specially endowed prophets, whose fiery messages to their people were intended for far more than their own times. At length, when the stage had been fully set, came the fullest development of God's self-disclosure and the completest form of the redemptive action of God. Jesus the Messiah came to be the 'Emmanuel', i.e. 'God with us.' Hence, God has down the ages revealed Himself in words and He has also revealed Himself in redemptive acts whether in relation to individuals or to the whole nation of Israel. At length His fuller revelation of Himself in Christ, which is complete so far as man's needs are concerned, is in the thought of the Bible raised to a supreme position.

III. FORMS IN WHICH GOD SPOKE TO MEN

The Bible indicates that God has chosen more than one form in which to make Himself known at different periods of history. In introducing the meaning of Christ's coming into the world, the Epistle to the Hebrews comments 'God, having of old time spoken unto the fathers in the prophets by divers portions and in divers manners, hath at the end of these days spoken unto us in his Son . . .' (Heb. i. 1, 2). Five distinct forms in which God revealed Himself to men are found in the Bible records. It is instructive briefly to glance at these:

a. Personal appearances

God is stated to have shown Himself to certain men under various physical and personal forms. E.g. in the Old Testament, Moses was met by God in the vision associated with the angel at the burning bush (Ex. iii. 2–6); Joshua saw the figure of a man—the Captain of the Lord's host—over against the city (Jos. v. 13–15); and angelic visitors appeared to men as in Gn. xvi. 10–13 and xxxi. 11. One such meeting is differently described (in Gn. xxxii. 24–30) and Jacob's comment is, 'I have seen God face to face, and my life is preserved.' Later Bible references often interpret these incidents. Two of these interpretations are worth noticing. (i) In Dt. xxxiv. 10, Moses is described as one 'whom the Lord knew face to face'; (2) in Nu. xii. 8, Moses is again described as having a very close relationship with God: 'With him will I speak mouth to mouth, even manifestly, and not in dark speeches; and the form of the Lord shall he behold: wherefore then were ye not afraid to speak against my servant, against

c

Moses?' Again, in Acts vi. 15 and vii. 55, in the case of Stephen, and for Paul in Acts ix. 3-6, unusual direct appearances of God are described.

b. Voices and Visions

There are a number of recorded instances of divine communications (in separation from other external phenomena) to the prophets either by an audible voice in a human language, by visions, or by suggestions made to the inner consciousness of the recipient. These communications are presented in the text of Scripture as something quite other than simply a heightening of what is ordinarily known as the 'inspiration', e.g. of a literary or an artistic genius. In almost all the cases which are cited in the Old and New Testaments there was no apparent or prior desire to receive or to search for such a communication on the part of the one to whom the voice or vision came. It 'came' supernaturally upon them, and in the majority of cases they are said to have shown signs of fear and to have expressed a desire to be relieved from the duty of announcing the message which had been imparted to them.

As examples of unusual communication may be cited God's approach to man: (i) *By voice*: Mt. i. 20, ii. 13, 19; (ii) *By dream*: Gn. xxxvii. 5 (to Joseph) and to Pharaoh's butler and baker (Gn. xl. 5); to Joseph, the fiancé of Mary (Mt. i. 20, and ii. 13) and to the Magi (Mt. ii. 12); (iii) *By vision*: much of what was written by both the major and minor prophets is presented as something 'seen' (cf. Is. vi. 1-13; Ezk. i. 1 and 4, and the book of Revelation); (iv) By some form of '*possession*'. With this may be compared 2 Pet. i. 20, 21, where the writers of the Old Testament Scriptures are described as those who were 'borne along' in the same way that a sailing ship is driven by the wind at sea. These men appear to have regarded themselves as simply God's instruments in a supernatural process of conveying God's will to men.

c. Miracles

In some instances God used miracle to reveal Himself. It is important, however, to notice the place and meaning of the miracles recorded in the Bible. Miracles are confined to four main eras of Israel's history: (i) the period between the exodus from Egypt and the entry into Canaan; (ii) the struggle with Baal worship in the days of Elijah and Elisha; (iii) the period of the exile; and (iv) the times of our Lord and of the Acts of the Apostles. They are variously described by Hebrew words, and their Greek equivalents, as 'wonders', 'powers', 'works of God' and 'signs'. The last-named provides us with the chief clue to their use by God as a means of revelation. In the main, miracles are signs given to faith. They confirm the already existing, though feeble, faith of believers. Some miracles, however, particularly in the case of our Lord, were designed as a sign of His divine mission. Jn. x. 37, 38 declares: 'If I do not the works of my Father, believe me not. But if I do them, though ye believe not me, believe the works: that ye may know and understand that the Father is in me, and I in the Father.' Cf. Jn. xv. 24. Similarly, a miraculous revelation was used to bring about Paul's conversion. It is described in Acts ix. 3–7 as follows: 'And as he journeyed, it came to pass that he drew nigh unto Damascus: and suddenly there shone round about him a light out of heaven: and he fell upon the earth, and heard a voice saying unto him, Saul, Saul, why persecutest thou me? And he said, Who art thou, Lord? And he said, I am Jesus whom thou persecutest: but rise, and enter into the city, and it shall be told thee what thou must do. And the men that journeyed with him stood speechless, hearing the voice, but beholding no man.'

d. A Supernatural Activity of God's Spirit

In the case of the writers of the books of Scripture, as will subsequently be discussed, the process of God's revelation is presented as being the result of an operation of God's Spirit moving and controlling the human minds of the writers. The process, therefore, is both divine and human. Professor B. B. Warfield in his writing on the biblical description of revelation uses the term 'the concursive operation' of God's Spirit.[1] The

---

[1] This chapter owes much, as do several others in the book, to the writings of Dr. B. B. Warfield, Professor of Didactic and Polemic Theology, Princeton Theological Seminary 1887–1921, and especially to his book *The Inspiration and Authority of the Bible* (Marshall, Morgan & Scott).

Holy Spirit employed the full powers of the human writers who were the organs of revelation. The personalities of these writers, however, were not superseded. They used historical research as St. Luke, or logical reason as St. Paul. The result is truly human and yet fully supernatural (1 Cor. ii. 13, xiv. 37). In the final analysis, however, the characteristic of revelation as described in Scripture itself is its essential supernaturalness. The inspiration is attributed directly to God from whom alone it derives its unique quality and authority.

e. The Son of God

Finally, the culminating point of God's self-disclosure is His coming to mankind in the Person of His Son. Towards Him the whole of the Old Testament moves forward and to Him the whole of the New Testament looks back. For this reason our Lord is in the Gospel of St. John called the 'Word', in John's first Epistle 'the Word of life' and in the Revelation 'the Word of God', because He is the focus of all that God wishes to say to men (Heb. i. 1-3). He is Himself the revelation (1 Cor. i. 30). As Professor B. B. Warfield comments: 'When this fact in all its meaning was made the possession of men revelation was completed, and in that sense ceased. Jesus Christ is no less the end of revelation than He is the end of the law. . . . The entirety of the New Testament is but the explanatory word accompanying and giving its effect to the fact of Christ.' The fact, however, would not mean much to us in our generation unless it had been *recorded* and explained for us. Only so could we know of the 'fact of Christ' and of His supreme sacrifice for us.

IV. AN OBJECTION TO THE USUAL DEFINITION

It is common in present-day theological discussions to speak as though the Bible contains a revelation of God only in the form of a record of historical redemptive acts. The Old and New Testaments are said to be simply the records, or the deposit of the witness of the prophets and the apostles to Christ. It is suggested that the Bible contains a minimum of direct statements concerning the being and nature of God, of Christ, and of man. In other words, it is claimed by some writers that the Bible does not provide us with definitive propositions which would enable us to state formally what God has been pleased to reveal, and from which it is possible to draw up a creed. Rather, it is said, the prophets of the Old Testament declared and described the mighty acts of God as they were again and again displayed in Israel's history and which are so triumphantly epitomized in some of the Psalms. Similarly, and so far as the New Testament is concerned, it is claimed that the apostles simply 'witnessed to' what they had seen and heard. This, of course, is distinctly stated in 1 Jn. i. 1–4: 'That which was from the beginning, that which we have heard, that which we have seen with our eyes, that which we beheld, and our hands handled, concerning the Word of life. . . .' Yet to affirm that such personal witness of the apostles is clearly a large part of the message of the New Testament is one thing, but it is quite another to go on to assert that this adequately represents the whole position.

It is a matter of no small practical importance. The very foundation of Christian doctrine as it has long been understood in the Church is involved. Earlier generations have constructed a biblical theology by means of careful exegesis and have assembled what to them were 'proof texts'. These were accepted as being based on directly inspired statement concerning crucial matters of faith and conduct. Most editions of the Westminster Confession have, for example, been furnished with such Scripture references. In the first half of this century there has been a general undervaluation of doctrine in the Church as a whole and a movement away from such an approach to biblical theology. More recently, a partial recovery of interest in doctrine has been accompanied by two divergent tendencies. One of these is apt to make sweeping doctrinal assertions in isolation from historical roots. The other is so concerned with the historical setting that it is in danger of doing violence to the content and divine authority of the revelation itself. Amongst devotees of the latter view are some who have been known to declare that there 'is no propositional revelation' in Holy Scripture!

The original aim of this school of thought would seem to have been the laudable and salutary one of taking issue with those who seemed about to cut loose from its historical roots all interpretation of the divine revelation. Now an excess of zeal for revelation *in deeds* has begun to take issue with revelation *in words*. As Scripture presents itself, God is seen to have revealed Himself both by mighty acts and also by prophetic words. The latter are frequently given to us (to use the terminology of logic) in the form of propositions and of direct speech. The issue represents a divergence between two concepts of (i) indirect and of (ii) direct forms of communication. Granted in each case a measure of 'inspiration' and 'religious genius' to the human writers, the two views yet lead to radically different results. There is all the difference between (i) a group of writers who were men of religious insight and who conceived themselves as simply interpreting their own and their nation's religious history, and (ii) a body of men who claimed that they were thinking God's thoughts and speaking God's words after Him.

We must not minimize the plain meaning of the accounts of its own nature which are provided by the Bible. The 'burdens' of the prophets of the Old Testament, the teaching of our Lord in the Gospels, and the Epistles of the New Testament contain a number of 'propositions' and direct statements concerning God and His will for men. It will be possible here to consider only some of them. The Law, given through Moses, is one form of the revelation of God's character and it is given in the form of direct statement. Much of predictive prophecy comes in the form of promise and direct statement concerning the future. The Sermon on the Mount (Mt. v–vii) is again a fuller revelation of the character of God and much of it is given in the form of propositions. It is hard to see how anyone can classify as purely 'revelation through history' such teaching as is given by our Lord in John's Gospel, or that of Paul in the doctrinal sections of his Epistles (e.g. 1 Cor. xv) or that in the Epistle to the Hebrews.[1] Such sweeping generalizations as that 'there is no propositional revelation,' which are much in vogue with a contemporary school of thought, are in conflict with the plain statements of the Bible (cf. 1 Cor. ii).

---

[1] The Epistle to the Hebrews contains also, in the catalogue of those heroes who displayed great faith (chapter xi), an example of teaching which is based on history.

V. THE ESSENTIAL CHARACTER OF REVELATION

It is important to note that it is as essential to the Bible's view of revelation to emphasize the supernatural nature of the means through which it has been acquired as the supernatural source from which it comes. God has made Himself and His gracious purposes known to man in an immediate and direct Word of God, which is reverently to be received by man. This authoritative message has not been attained by human effort. It must simply be received. In fact, this giving of the revelation and the process of enshrining it in a written record is to be viewed as a part of the redemptive work of God. Modern thought resists such a view. It declines to grant the reality of such a process and dislikes the proposition that the minds of the writers of the Bible were necessarily receptive ('passive') before the divine control and it questions knowledge which is said to have been imparted solely on the divine initiative. Numerous theories have been propounded to account for the phenomenon of the Bible by some lower process. But we must insist, with Professor B. B. Warfield, that 'the organs of revelation occupy a receptive attitude. The contents of their messages are not something thought out, inferred, hoped for or feared by them, but are something conveyed to them, often forced upon them, by the irresistible might of the revealing Spirit.'

The nature of revelation is best illustrated by such words of the prophet Isaiah: 'In the year that king Uzziah died I saw the Lord sitting upon a throne, high and lifted up, and his train filled the temple. . . . Then said I, Woe is me! for I am undone; because I am a man of unclean lips, and I dwell in the midst of a people of unclean lips: for mine eyes have seen the King, the Lord of hosts' (Is. vi. 1, 5). Jeremiah is emphatic concerning his need for words to be given him: 'Now the word of the Lord came to me, saying, Before I formed thee . . . I knew thee, and before thou camest forth out of the womb I sanctified thee; I have appointed thee a prophet unto the nations. Then said I, Ah, Lord God! behold, I cannot speak: for I am a child. But the Lord said unto me, Say not, I am a child: . . . Then the Lord put forth his hand, and touched my mouth; and the Lord said unto me, Behold, I have put my words in thy mouth' (Je. i. 4–9).

CHAPTER FOUR

THE FIRST DOCUMENTS

THE self-revelation which God gave to patriarch and to prophet in the Old Testament and, through our Lord, to the apostles in the New Testament, could have had little influence on our needs today if we were not in possession of some permanent and reliable record of what was communicated to them. Subsequent generations have stood in need of one of three things—an accurate oral tradition (which, however, is difficult to preserve); an accurately written document (which is easier to preserve); or a series of similar and continuous day-to-day communications. God has chosen the second means. The first chapter of the Westminster Confession, after discussing God's revelation of Himself to His people, continues—'and afterwards, for the better preserving and propagating of the truth, and for the more sure establishment and comfort of the Church . . . (it pleased the Lord) to commit the same wholly unto writing, which maketh the Holy Scripture to be most necessary; those former ways of God's revealing His will unto His people being now ceased.' For us in the twentieth century the records must necessarily be the focal point of interest. What, therefore, do these original documents claim for themselves?

I. THE OLD TESTAMENT

The data concerning the nature of revelation, which are presented for the case of the Old Testament, are found in the form of (i) the comparatively few and sparing comments of the Old Testament writers and (ii) the statements which the New Testament writers, in retrospect, have made concerning it. Some minds find it difficult to attribute the same degree of credibility and reputation for accuracy to the Old Testament, which they are usually prepared (on the evidence) to accord to the New Testament. Yet we must remind ourselves repeatedly that our Lord and the New Testament writers make very strong claims for the Old Testament. Our first aim, however, will be to look at what the Old Testament writers say concerning their own writings. It will be convenient to classify the books into four groups: (a) the Pentateuch (i.e. the first five books), whose authorship is attributed by later Old Testament books and by the New Testament to Moses, the Law-giver; (b) the Historical Books, in which is found the subsequent history of Israel; (c) the Poetical 'Writings', of which the greater part is attributed to David and Solomon; and (d) the Major and Minor Prophets.

a. The Pentateuch

The Pentateuch has importance far beyond its immediate setting, not only because, as the 'Book of the Law', it is repeatedly referred to, and treated with such great respect by subsequent writers in the Old Testament, but because of its use in the New Testament. These important documents are referred to as 'the book of the law of Moses' as early as Jos. i. 7, 8 and as late as Dn. ix. 11–13. There are numerous references which indicate that these first books of the Old Testament were greatly revered and that Moses was regarded as the greatest of the prophets. To cite from Deuteronomy (whose Mosaic authorship, at least in the present form of the book, some modern scholars have found difficult to accept) we have such a typical statement as in Dt. xxxi. 9, 25, 26, 'And Moses wrote this law, and delivered it unto the priests the sons of Levi . . . saying, Take this book of the law, and put it by the side of the ark of the covenant of the Lord your God.' Not only did Israel later treat the whole of the Pentateuch as the 'Book of the Law' or as 'the Law of Moses', but almost interchangeably as 'the book of the law of God' (cf. Jos. xxiv. 26). We are introduced to these books in such phrases as: 'And Moses wrote all the words of the Lord . . . And he took the book of the covenant, and read in the audience of the people: and they said, All that the Lord hath spoken will we do, and be obedient' (Ex. xxiv. 4, 7). Glancing at the chapters of the books of Exodus and Leviticus we find the majority of the sections commence with such phrases as 'And the Lord spake unto Moses, saying . . .' Similarly, the law of Sinai itself is prefaced by the words: 'And God spake these words and said . . .' The writer obviously expected his readers to accept these oft repeated prefaces at their face value, that is, to accept the fact that God really *did* speak to Moses and *did* give him the contents of the book of the covenant. Many other parts of the Pentateuch are introduced by similar words. Let us, therefore, remind ourselves, again, of the comment in Nu. xii. 7, 8, on Moses' relationship with God. Whereas God had been prepared to speak to other contemporary prophets in a vision, He says 'My servant Moses is not so; he is faithful in all mine house: with him will I speak mouth to mouth, even manifestly, and not in dark speeches; and the form of the Lord shall he behold.'

In the subsequent book (Jos. xxiv. 26) there is the interesting comment that Joshua also wrote a section which was added to 'the book of the law of God', but *(in loco)* this would appear to be simply the covenant made in Shechem. It might, however, mean a part of the book, or the whole book, which bears Joshua's name. The veneration in which the law was held is exemplified throughout the Old Testament, but particularly in the Psalms. Cf. Pss. i, xix, cxix, etc., and *'By the word of thy lips* I have kept me from the ways of the violent' (Ps. xvii. 4).

b. The Historical Books

The historical books of the Old Testament present their contents in a factual manner and their writers obviously expect their statements to be regarded as true history. The authors at certain places have given the information that they have made use of Israel's official State archives and other contemporary records. From certain references outside the Bible and parallels in 2 Kings and Chronicles it is believed that the line of prophets kept a candid and critical record of events which was regarded in some way as official. This fact may account for the variations, where the prophetic archives differed in viewpoint from the State records. It has been claimed that such information from the official 'Book of the Chronicles of the kings of Israel' has been utilized at least thirty times in the two books of Kings and also repeatedly in the two books of the Chronicles.

In none of these books do the writers actually comment that their means of inspiration, or special knowledge, has been received directly from God. It must, however, be remembered that the priests and leaders of a people, which was outstandingly scrupulous in such matters, welcomed these books alongside the sacred Law and treated them as belonging to their sacred Scriptures. This in itself is significant and must not be lightly set aside.

c. The Poetical Books

The poetical books, again, are reticent concerning the nature of the source of the poets' illumination and their authority for speaking. What is written, however, is a direct presentation of what is obviously regarded as having been imparted by God to the writer. Israel, at the time of our Lord, our Lord Himself, and the apostles all accept without question their authority, making citations from most of those books, and especially from the Psalms, in the same way as from the other 'Holy Writings'. We shall notice later that our Lord does not hesitate to say: 'David, *speaking by the Holy Ghost.*' A key statement is presented by 2 Sa. xxiii. 1, 2, and it is instructive to note carefully what is said: 'Now these be the last words of David. David the son of Jesse saith, . . . The spirit of the Lord spake by me, and his word was upon my tongue.' The late Professor W. Sanday comments that in the Psalms 'there are a number of instances in which the Psalmist adopts forms of language which we are accustomed to associate specially with prophecy' (*Inspiration*, p. 195).

In the book of Proverbs are to be found several such statements, e.g. the voice of Wisdom in chapters i. 20—ii. 22: 'Wisdom crieth . . . Behold, I will pour out my spirit unto you . . . Then shalt thou understand the fear of the Lord, and find the knowledge of God. For the Lord giveth wisdom.' Also, at the commencement of chapters xxx and xxxi will be found references to 'the oracle', or 'the burden', which follows. The chapters which follow are given in the form normally used by the prophets of Israel for one of their special messages. The Hebrew word translated 'oracle' or 'burden' probably conveys the basic idea of 'to speak with groans', i.e. under compulsion or constraint. The thought conveyed is that of men who are driven on by God to speak hard things which they would rather omit. It is a

word which in Scripture is used only of God speaking directly
or through a prophet.

d. The Prophets

When we examine the prophetic writings of the Old Testament,
we are again confronted by a method of introduction, which is
reminiscent of the phrases used in the Pentateuch: 'The Lord
spake unto Moses, saying . . .' Sections of these prophecies are
repeatedly introduced: 'Thus saith the Lord . . .' 'The word of
the Lord came unto me . . .' 'Thus the Lord Jehovah showed
me . . .' It is obvious that here again the writer expects these
words to be taken at their face value. The prophets are frequently conscious that they were called, often much against their
wills, to serve their generation by prophesying. They name the
time when they were summoned to the unwelcome duty from
which they naturally shrank (cf. Is. vi; Je. i; Ezk. iii. 14). Their
descriptions make it apparent that they were impelled by a
vivid awareness that they had been visited by God in a very
direct manner, and that they were under constraint to announce
what they had seen and heard. Also, they make it clear that they
did not themselves always understand what they heard and
wrote—e.g. Daniel writes: ' I heard, but I understood not:
then said I, O my lord, what shall be the issue of these things?
And he said, Go thy way, Daniel: for the words are shut up and
sealed till the time of the end' (Dn. xii. 8, 9). This statement
should be compared with the explanation found in 1 Pet. i.
10–12: 'Concerning which salvation the prophets sought and
searched diligently . . . searching what time . . . the Spirit
of Christ which was in them did point unto . . . To whom it
was revealed, that not unto themselves, but unto you, did they
minister these things.'

It is, further, instructive to note the importance which the
prophets place upon the nature of their message. They clearly
distinguish what was imparted to them by God from thoughts
which may arise in their own minds. There is a significant
contrast between 'Then the Lord put forth his hand, and touched
my mouth; and the Lord said unto me, Behold, I have put my
words in thy mouth' (Je. i. 9) and the false prophets, who 'pro-

phesy unto you a lying vision, and divination, and a thing of nought, and the deceit of their own heart' (cf. Ezk. xiii. 1–7). The prophets are emphatic that they do not speak their own words or act upon their own initiative—but they speak simply because God has commanded them to do so. Amos announces, 'Surely the Lord God will do nothing, but he revealeth his secret unto his servants the prophets. The lion hath roared, who will not fear? the Lord God hath spoken, who can but prophesy?' (Am. iii. 7, 8). Cf. Je. xx. 7–9 and Ezk. iii. 4–12.

Numerous other examples could be added, but space dictates that attention should be given to only one further series of illuminating passages in the Prophets. Some of the writers apparently knew that they were recording divine prophecies for the benefit of later generations. Such would clearly appear to be the case in Je. xxxvi. 27 and 32 and Ezk. xxvi, xxvii, xxxi, xxxii, xxxviii and xxxix. The prophet Isaiah, in xxxiv. 16, states that what he has written is to be regarded as 'the book of the Lord'. In some of his prophecies God is represented as speaking directly, e.g. in Is. x. 12 and xix. 2. When we come to the Minor Prophets, this is repeatedly the case, as e.g. the remarkable passage in Hosea which begins, 'O Ephraim, what shall I do unto thee? O Judah, what shall I do unto thee? . . . for I desire mercy, and not sacrifice; and the knowledge of God more than burnt offerings' (Ho. vi. 4–11). See also Zc. ix. 1–7 and xii. 9, 10. In short, most of the prophets announce their 'burdens' as being in the nature of direct statements of God.

II. THE NEW TESTAMENT

a. New Testament References to the older 'Holy Writings'

When the collection of these first sacred documents was finally complete, the whole body of books became referred to (in the Greek New Testament) as 'The Scriptures' (*hai graphai*, e.g. in Lk. xxiv. 27) or, sometimes, the term is used 'The Holy Writings' (*ta hiera grammata*, e.g. 2 Tim. iii. 15). When referring to the Old Testament books or making a quotation from them, no difference is made in respect of their validity in the New Testament. They are treated alike as equally authoritative.

It is also of significance to notice the comments of the New Testament writers when referring to the writings and the writers of the Old Testament. Three 'classic' passages leave us in no doubt about the views of our Lord and the apostles concerning the nature and authority of the earlier documents.

1. St. Paul, in describing the 'Holy Scriptures', comments, 'All scripture is given by inspiration of God' (2 Tim. iii. 16 AV; see the whole context verses 14–17). In the Greek New Testament the operative word in this sentence is *theopneustos* which is translated in the Authorized Version 'given by inspiration', the literal equivalent being 'God-breathed'. In view of the adjectival form of this word and the omission of the copulative verb, the English Revised Version has translated the phrase 'Every scripture inspired of God is also profitable.' The inference which some have made from the R.V. translation is that certain of the Scriptures may be regarded as specially inspired by God and therefore profitable, whereas other Scriptures might not be in the same category. This is not, however, what the R.V. intends to say. The A.V. asserts the inspiration of all Scripture; the R.V. assumes it. It is interesting to notice that the recently published revision of the American Revised Standard Version has replaced the form given originally in the Authorized Version, viz., 'All scripture is inspired of God.'

One of the most careful studies of the subject has been made by the late Professor B. B. Warfield of Princeton Theological Seminary in 'God-inspired Scripture'.[1] He shows conclusively that all words compounded with 'pneustos' have a passive sense as originally used and that the passage in Timothy can bear no other meaning than that the words of Scripture are regarded as 'having been breathed by God'. A more accurate English equivalent would be 'spiration' or 'ex-piration', rather than 'in-spiration'. In other words, it suggests that Scripture represents a process in which a revelation has been breathed *out* from God

[1] Originally published as an article and included with an article 'Inspiration' from the Int. Stand. Bible Encyclopaedia, in the volume *Revelation and Inspiration*, Oxford University Press (U.S.A.). This book has recently been re-published in this country under the title *The Inspiration and Authority of Scripture* (Marshall, Morgan & Scott).

and the emphasis is upon a divine operation. This divine action is attributed to all the Scriptures. The whole process is regarded as a deliberate divine action, for God's 'breath', in the thought of the Bible, is a demonstration of His power (cf. Ps. xxxiii. 6). The context makes it abundantly clear that the writer is intending to emphasize the fact that Timothy is intimately acquainted with the Holy Scriptures, which are able to make him wise unto salvation, and that 'every scripture, because it is God-breathed, is also profitable' for the purposes which he goes on to list. In other words, Paul the apostle emphasizes that Scripture is the result of a special act of God, and the overmastering inference is therefore that it has *unique* value for the various purposes outlined.

2. Peter[1] also makes certain references to the Old Testament Scriptures which may be regarded as the complement of the above: 'No prophecy of scripture is of private interpretation. For no prophecy ever came by the will of man: but men spake from God, being moved by the Holy Ghost' (2 Pet. i. 20, 21). In the American Revised Standard Version the passage is translated: 'First of all you must understand this, that no prophecy of scripture is a matter of one's own interpretation, because no prophecy ever came by the impulse of man, but men moved by the Holy Spirit spoke from God.'

Before it is possible to make any inference from these two statements it is necessary to determine to what the phrase 'prophecy of scripture' (verse 20) refers. Since Moses, the lawgiver, is regarded in New Testament times not only as the lawgiver but also as the greatest of the prophets, do the words refer to the whole body of Old Testament Scripture, which is collectively termed 'prophetic', i.e. is described by its major characteristic? Or, does it refer only to those parts of Scripture which we regard as specially prophetic in the restricted sense of bearing a special revelation for those coming later in history? The total context (reading from verse 16, 'For we did not follow cunningly devised fables . . .') and the general nature of the immediate reference suggests that we should be correct in

---

[1] The writer takes the view that the apostle was the author of 2 Peter (see page 114).

accepting the phrase as applying to the whole body of the Old Testament Scripture. These earlier writings seem to be elsewhere in Scripture referred to, in a general manner, as 'prophetic'.

Then the context, also, goes on to emphasize that it has *never* (Gk. *ou . . . pote*) happened that a man has by his own will produced a true prophecy. The very word 'moved', which is used to describe the force which drove on the writers in their tasks, suggests that their human wills remained passive. They were 'moved', or more literally 'borne'. The Greek *pherō* suggests that the human instruments were 'borne' along at the will of another Person and to an end determined by this other Person. Much as sailing ships are driven along by the wind, so the human penmen were carried forward in their prophetic writing by the Holy Spirit who is described in biblical language as the mighty 'breath' or 'wind' of God. The total effect of the whole passage, therefore, is to give an impression of the trustworthiness of 'the prophetic word' (primarily, in this particular context, concerning the deity of Christ) because it is of divine origin. Professor Warfield comments 'Because this is the way every prophecy of Scripture has been brought, it affords a more sure basis of confidence than even the testimony of eye-witnesses.'

3. In Jn. x. 34 ff. our Lord makes the statement 'the scripture cannot be broken' which, we suggest (especially in view of the context), can be understood in no other way than as asserting the complete reliability of the Old Testament Scriptures. It is reliable because of its divine origin. If we are to accept His authority in such matters, then we must accord full respect to the body of writings which He accepted in His earthly lifetime as they were found in the places of worship of His nation. No recorded word of His suggests anything to the contrary than that He expected His disciples to share His own attitude in these matters.

b. The New Testament References to its Own Nature

There is, however, the second body of writings—the New Testament. Let us examine the internal references to their own nature. These additional documents are, with few important exceptions, stated to have been written by apostles. Even the exceptions give ample indication that they were written by those who had enjoyed close relations with the apostles, and had benefited from their first-hand knowledge. In general, therefore, the usefulness and importance of these writings depend upon the accuracy of the apostolic company in their specially appointed function of bearing witness to the facts of the life, death, resurrection and ascension of our Lord. Their reliability also depends upon the power of the various writers to impart positive doctrinal teaching which they claim to bear the divine authority. In fact, they introduce their writings in such a way as to imply that their contents, which were recorded subsequent to our Lord's ascension, are to be accepted alongside the other Holy Writings and to be accorded an equal place with them.

First, there is what *prima facie* would seem to be an unequivocal statement by Peter (assuming that he wrote 2 Peter) that the Epistles of Paul which were extant in the lifetime of the other apostles, were already being given equal honour with the Old Testament. The actual words are: 'Even as our beloved brother Paul also, according to the wisdom given to him, wrote unto you; as also in all his epistles, speaking in them of these things; wherein are some things hard to be understood, which the ignorant and unstedfast wrest, as they do also the other scriptures, unto their own destruction' (2 Pet. iii. 15, 16). By the phrase 'the other scriptures' it is difficult to imagine that Peter is here referring to anything other than the Old Testament Scriptures upon which he has already drawn heavily in earlier references and citations in this same Epistle. We may compare with this Paul's statement: 'If any man thinketh himself to be a prophet, or spiritual, let him take knowledge of the things which I write unto you, that they are the commandment of the Lord' (1 Cor. xiv. 37). Further reference will be made to the authority which the apostles claim, directly or by implication, for their writings in Chapter vi. (see p. 70).

c. The Writers of the Gospels

For the remainder of this chapter we shall confine ourselves to the chief direct allusions to the nature of their writings which have been bequeathed by the New Testament authors. In the

D

Gospels we have only two important references, and these are confined to Luke and John. In the preface to his Gospel, Luke indicates that he set out, in view of the considerable number of such narratives coming into circulation, (i) to provide an authoritative and accurate account of the life and death of Christ, since he had access to the invaluable help of well-known and accurate eye witnesses; and (ii) to do it in such a way that Theophilus might 'know the certainty concerning the things' which apparently he had so far received only in oral form (Lk. i. 1–4). It so happens that Luke, a physician, does not name himself in either the Gospel or the Acts, both of which are commonly attributed to him. However, the tradition which assigns them to him has much internal confirmatory support. In any case, the writer claims that he is in a very good position to secure accuracy. Assuming that the writer is Luke, then his known intimacy with the apostles suggests that this very accurate and trained observer would have been able to attain his aim of producing a valid record.[1]

John, who is even more reticent concerning his own part in the production of the manuscript, and also does not directly name himself, states his object in writing as follows: 'Many other signs therefore did Jesus in the presence of the disciples, which are not written in this book: but these are written, that ye may believe that Jesus is the Christ,[2] the Son of God; and that believing ye may have life in his name' (Jn. xx. 30, 31). In the Gospels we find no special claim by the writers that they received divine aid in their authorship. They are so confident of the truth

---

[1] Amongst others, one well-known scholar, Sir William Ramsay, has provided much evidence which demonstrates the meticulous accuracy of Luke's writing; cf. *Luke the Physician* (William Ramsay). See also *Luke the Historian in the Light of Research* (A. T. Robertson).

[2] A great deal of inspiration tends to be lost by readers of the New Testament who see in the word 'Christ' only a proper name, as is the personal name Jesus, rather than recognizing it as the chief official title. Few English readers today, when reading in the Epistles the phrase 'our Lord Jesus Christ', are able to feel the force and thrill of its meaning at the time of writing, i.e. that He, Jesus of Nazareth, is (i) 'redeemer of His people,' (ii) the 'anointed king' (fulfilling God's promise to Israel), and (iii) 'our Lord,' i.e. of the Church and of the individual.

of their writings that their records concerning Jesus, the Messiah, are left to speak for themselves.

d. New Testament Anonymous Books

In the Acts of the Apostles, Luke (the presumed writer who, in several places, uses the first personal pronoun 'we' in this book) provides a preface which is similar in style to that which is found at the beginning of his Gospel. It is also—as the preface to the Gospel—addressed to Theophilus. In this second volume, when referring to the evidences for his statements, there is a new emphasis upon Christ's 'commandment (given) through the Holy Ghost unto the apostles' and the 'many proofs' which had been provided in confirmation of 'the things concerning the kingdom of God' (Acts i. 1–3). Again, the inference is inescapable that the reader is expected to accept at their face value the historical facts provided concerning the earliest expansion of the Church and to treat those documents as accurate and authoritative. There is one further anonymous book in the New Testament, the Epistle to the Hebrews, in which Luke's hand may have had a part. Tradition ascribes this anonymous letter to Paul. Eusebius (*Eccl. Hist.* vi. 14) quotes Clement of Alexandria as affirming that Paul wrote the Epistle in Hebrew (or Aramaic) and that Luke translated it into Greek. Modern speculation, however, has suggested various other authors. Of these (in view of Heb. xiii. 22–25) Luke, or one of the other companions of Paul during his imprisonment, are the most likely. Perhaps the best comment which has yet been made on the subject of its authorship is that of Origen: 'As to who wrote the Epistle to the Hebrews, God alone knows the truth.' The matter is perhaps better left at that.

e. The Epistles and Revelation

With the exception of the three which are attributed to John, each of the apostolic letters (or 'Epistles') and the book of 'the Revelation' is prefaced with the name of the apostle who wrote it. Almost all of such letters call attention to the validity of the writer's apostleship, and therefore emphasize the authority of his commission to teach and to write. Occasionally the writers have referred to the influence of a power outside of themselves and they claim that they speak under the control of the Holy Spirit. For example, Paul unambiguously declares 'We impart this (i.e. the understanding of God's gifts) in words not taught by human wisdom but taught by the Spirit' (1 Cor. ii. 13 R.S.V.). The whole of the second chapter of the first Epistle to the Corinthians will repay study from this point of view. With Paul's assertions may be compared the following phrase of Peter —'these things which now have been announced unto you through them that preached the gospel unto you through the Holy Ghost' (1 Pet. i. 12). Similarly, when Paul is engaged in reproving the fickleness of the Corinthian church he adds that if he again comes to Corinth, he will not be prepared to speak smoothly to those who were opposing his apostolic authority— 'since you desire proof that *Christ is speaking in me*' (2 Cor. xiii. 3 R.S.V.). Whereas in the case of the Thessalonians he is able to say 'our gospel came to you not only in word, but also in power and in the Holy Spirit and with full conviction' (1 Thes. i. 5 R.S.V.). One of the clearest of all Paul's references to the meaning of his God-given authority is where he reminds the Galatians that he did not receive his gospel from any human source, 'but it came to me through revelation of Jesus Christ' (Gal. i. 12).

John, in his first Epistle, claims to write under a special and intimate knowledge of the Lord Christ whom he had seen and actually touched. He introduces the main part of his message with the words 'This is the message which we have heard *from him*, and announce unto you' (1 Jn. i. 5). He confidently expects them fully to accept and to appreciate what he writes, because 'the anointing (i.e. the Holy Spirit's presence) which ye received of him abideth in you . . . his anointing teacheth you concerning all things' (1 Jn. ii. 27). In the book of the Revelation the same apostle claims that what is recorded came from Jesus Christ who 'made it known by sending his angel to his servant John' (Rev. i. 1 R.S.V.). It is difficult to imagine how any candid reader of the New Testament can resist the total impression which writer after writer conveys. They all obviously regarded themselves as specially appointed and specially authorized men who were writing under the constraint of the Holy Spirit in order to give a factually true account of what the ascended Lord Jesus Christ desired to be known concerning Himself and His kingdom. Nowhere do we find the claim of authority made in bolder terms than when Paul writes: 'by revelation was made known unto me the mystery, as I wrote afore in few words, whereby, when ye read, ye can perceive my understanding in the mystery of Christ; which in other generations was not made known unto the sons of men, as it hath now been revealed unto his holy apostles and prophets in the Spirit' (Eph. iii. 3–5).

CHAPTER FIVE

THE COMPLETION OF THE DOCUMENTS

FURTHER questions begin to present themselves. It may well be asked: 'Granted that the documents of Holy Scripture are appointed by God to convey to us the revelation of His being and of His acts of redemption towards mankind, what are the boundaries of the divine library which is available for our instruction?' Are there any books which have come to be treated as authoritative and have been included in the 'official' collection when they really deserve no such honour? Conversely, have certain books, which merited inclusion, found themselves finally excluded, or even been lost?

The problem is usually referred to as that of the completion of 'the Canon'. This word is a transliteration of the Greek *kanōn*, which means a measuring rod, or a rule. The term was applied originally not to a *complete* list of books but, rather, to the rule by which the basic teaching of the Christian faith was to be known, i.e. to a group of doctrines such as those which are formulated in the Apostles' Creed. The word in this sense appears in the Greek of Phil. iii. 16 (Textus Receptus): 'Let us walk by the same rule.' The underlying principle in the process of completing the Canon in the case of the New Testament was that since the apostles were the duly appointed instructors of the Church, its rule of faith must be looked for in the sum of their official teaching. Since also the essence of this teaching was to be found in their authentic didactic writings, these were collected into the acknowledged body of apostolic writings. The term 'Canon' later became commonly employed to refer to the completed catalogue of books in the New Testament. Those books which are included in the two completed lists—the Old[1] and the New Testaments—are referred to as

[1] *The Journal of Theological Studies* (January–April, 1948, pp. 17 ff.) presents an interesting case for the growth of the Old Testament Canon through three stages; i.e. (i) Law, (ii) Prophets, and (iii) Writings.

'Canonical'. Certain other ancient books which were in circulation, and which were included neither by the Jews in the Old Testament 'Canon', nor by the early Christian Church in the New Testament 'Canon', were termed 'Apocryphal' (i.e. 'hidden'), and these were regarded as not having the authority of Holy Scripture. Our immediate interest here is to notice the grounds on which the early Christian Church recognized whether or not a book should be regarded as a part of Holy Scripture. The problem is one which may be approached along three main lines: (i) there are a few scattered references within the books of Scripture to a completed body of writings; (ii) there is a limited amount of external historical evidence; and (iii) there is the fact of the inherent authority, which is carried by the books themselves. It is primarily upon the ground of its inherent authority that the main stream of orthodoxy in the Christian Church has, and must, base its claims for the Canon of Scripture. The closing section of this chapter will be devoted to a consideration of this important matter.

I. THE OLD TESTAMENT CANON

The Old Testament contains several suggestions that the contents of the Pentateuch received an official recognition. E.g. Ex. xxiv. 3, 4; Dt. xxxi. 11, 24–26; Jos. i. 7, 8; 1 Ki. ii. 3; 2 Ch. xxiii. 18. Similarly, at the close of the second section of the Psalms appears the phrase 'The prayers of David the son of Jesse are ended' (Ps. lxxii. 20). But the grounds and evidence upon which finally the completed Canon was recognized by Israel's spiritual leaders are not known. The basic consideration, derived from the internal evidence of Scripture itself, must therefore be that the Lord and His disciples acknowledged the Canon of the Old Testament as it was already accepted in their day. Whilst freely charging the scribes and Pharisees with 'making the word of God of none effect' by the intrusion of their traditional comments, our Lord never accused them of omitting, or taking from, the collection of writings. If we would follow our Lord and the apostles, we shall accept the Old Testament Canon as that which was accepted by the Jewish synagogue of their day.

That the Jewish synagogue in our Lord's day was using a Hebrew Bible identical with that known to us today would appear from the comprehensive reference to the martyrs of the Old Testament in Lk. xi. 51, which suggests that the Jewish Canon of the day similarly ended with 2 Chronicles. The external evidence is that there was little dispute concerning the extent of the Old Testament Canon at any period of Jewish history for which there are adequate relevant records. The collection of Old Testament Scriptures (which tradition states was officially made and promulgated by Ezra after the return from the exile in Babylon) was apparently not questioned. The Greek translation of the Old Testament Scriptures, the Septuagint, includes in Greek several of the apocryphal writings which arose in the district of Alexandria but none of these appear to have been recognized in the circles of Palestine. There is no evidence that official Judaism ever accepted the Apocrypha as canonical either in Palestine or Alexandria. So far as we know it was first accorded canonical status by the Greek-speaking church and has continued to enjoy that status throughout Greek (and also Latin) Christendom.

II. THE NEW TESTAMENT CANON

a. External evidence

When we approach the New Testament the position is somewhat different, though, here again, we are provided with little direct internal evidence. Many of the books in the New Testament were in the first instance addressed to widely separated churches. Time necessarily elapsed before their true nature and authority was universally recognized in other churches situated at a distance. The first recorded conscious attempt to define the books of the completed New Testament is the Muratorian 'Canon' made about A.D. 175, giving the names of the books received in Rome. Also a similar specification was made by Origen about the year A.D. 230. There is no clear historical record of an Oecumenical Council's having discussed this matter. It is doubtful if the list sometimes associated with the Council of Laodicea (held in A.D. 364) is more than the first official catalogue of the books *already* recognized by the churches as canonical.[1] Again, although the books of our present New Testament can be found widely quoted in the works of the 'ante-Nicene Fathers', the first completed New Testament catalogue was that which was offered by Eusebius (who died about A.D. 340). He provides a list of recognized books in his *Ecclesiastical History* (Book iii. 27). Since Eusebius is noted for scholarly care, his evidence must be regarded with due deference. He provides a collection of the titles of those books which were in his day unanimously and universally accepted as New Testament Scripture in the churches. It includes all of the books on the Contents Page of our present New Testament, with the exception of the following which he describes as 'accepted by the majority of churches.' The list of uncertain books names six of our present New Testament Epistles—Hebrews, James, 2 Peter, 2 and 3 John and Jude. Eusebius is equivocal concerning the book of the Revelation.

However, the reason for there being doubt in the case of these books is instructive. The difficulty seems to have arisen because these six Epistles do not contain an express statement that they came from the hands of one of the apostles or (as in the case of 2 and 3 John) they are addressed to an obscure individual. It needs to be commented that such an attitude augurs well for an approach to our problem. For the very care with which a book was scrutinized by the early Church for signs of its apostolic authority gives the greatest possible confidence that no unworthy book would easily have gained admittance and the very care with which everything of apostolic authority was preserved renders it unlikely that any valuable apostolic Epistle has been unnecessarily lost. From the beginning, the accepted books were publicly and constantly read in the churches. Any insufficiently accredited books would have stood a small chance of survival as authoritative. The danger would seem to have been the opposite one of possible loss of a true canonical book.

---

[1] Bishop Westcott has demonstrated that the list is absent from the Latin Version and three Syriac MSS, and that it was therefore probably a later addition.

b. Internal evidence

Of the internal evidence, we will select the most important as follows.

1. As already mentioned in a former chapter, Luke took great care to secure due apostolic information when writing his two books—the Gospel and the Acts. Similarly, John emphasizes in the preface to his Epistle that he has had the closest possible contact with both our Lord and the other apostles (see page 52).

2. Paul is careful to affix his personal signature to the letters which are being sent to be read out in the churches. For example, we read such references as 'The salutation of me Paul with mine own hand' (1 Cor. xvi. 21 and Col. iv. 18), and 'the salutation of me Paul with mine own hand, *which is the token in every epistle*' (2 Thes. iii. 17).

3. In the Epistle to the Colossians, Paul states: 'And when this epistle hath been read among you, cause that it be read also in the church of the Laodiceans; and that ye also read the epistle from Laodicea' (Col. iv. 16). No Epistle to the Laodiceans is known under that name. This may, however, not mean that a canonical 'Epistle to the Laodiceans' has been lost. The more likely explanation is that the original (or a copy) of one of his other letters (e.g. that to the Ephesians) was 'on circuit' and was due to arrive next from Laodicea to Colosse on its appointed journey round a group of churches. It is to be noted, of course, that by far the greatest part of Paul's correspondence has been lost. Only that which in the providence of God has been required for the guidance of the later ages of the Church has survived.

4. John, at the close of the Revelation, gives a stern warning to any who should desire to 'add unto' or 'take away from the words of the book of this prophecy' (Rev. xxii. 18, 19). In its immediate context this warning, of course, refers only to the book of Revelation.

III. THE LOSS OF THE AUTOGRAPH COPIES

There is, however, a further question of importance. It presents one of the biggest difficulties felt by many present-day students.

Early Israel, for a time, possessed the original copies of the Law and the Prophets and the first generation in the Christian Church was in possession of autograph copies of the apostolic letters. Today, however, we are in the position of being compelled to rely upon copies (or, indeed, copies of copies) of the originals. In the case of several books it is possible that we may only have copies of earlier copies of what are Greek translations of Aramaic originals. In any case, modern Christians in all lands have in the main to rely upon the current translations into the vernaculars of their respective countries. Can we then be sure of having anything approaching the *ipsissima verba* of the Holy Spirit? Can we rightly talk as if we had the very words of God?

It is not possible within the limits of this book adequately to discuss the long process of transmission of the text of the original Scriptures down to our day. For the student who desires to make a special study of the matter, we would refer to an up-to-date and admirable treatise, *The Books and the Parchments*, by F. F. Bruce.[1] We may, perhaps, be permitted to borrow two of Mr. Bruce's conclusions. Commenting upon the care with which the Hebrew scribes copied their MSS and the facilities for comparison with the later extant Hebrew texts, which are provided by Jerome's Latin translation of the Old Testament (about 400 A.D.), the Syriac Version (early in the Christian era) and the Greek Septuagint Version, he adds, 'Although the Septuagint text sometimes deviates from the Massoretic text and occasionally helps us to correct it, yet in general it confirms that no serious changes were introduced into the text of the Old Testament during the thousand years between the time when this (Septuagint) Version was made and the time to which our chief Hebrew MSS belong.' The recent discovery near Jericho of a Hebrew scroll of Isaiah, so far dated in the first (or second) century B.C.,[2] enables an even stronger statement to be made in the case of this section of the prophets.

[1] Mr. Bruce is head of the Department of Biblical Studies, University of Sheffield. The book is published by Pickering & Inglis at 12s. 6d.

[2] Some scholars do not accept a B.C. date. But even if their first or second century A.D. dating be correct, there is still very much earlier confirmation for the Hebrew text of Isaiah, and small sections of the Minor Prophets, than has hitherto been available.

In the case of the text of the New Testament Mr. Bruce is able to be more emphatic. Commenting on the many possibilities of error in the copying of MSS, he says: 'In view of the inevitable accumulation of such errors over so many centuries, it may be thought that the original texts of the New Testament documents have been corrupted beyond restoration. Some writers, indeed, insist on the likelihood of this to such a degree that one sometimes suspects they would be glad if it were so. But they are mistaken. There is no body of ancient literature in the world which enjoys such a wealth of good textual attestation as the New Testament.' Mr. Bruce ends his comments on this subject by reference to the work of the scholar who has in recent years done most in relation to the problem of transmission: 'There is no greater authority in this field of New Testament textual criticism than Sir Frederic Kenyon, and we may take his words to heart with confidence:

"It is reassuring at the end to find that the general result of all these discoveries and all this study is to strengthen the proof of the authenticity of the Scriptures, and our conviction that we have in our hands in substantial integrity, the veritable Word of God. . . . The interval then between the dates of original composition and the earliest extant evidence becomes so small as to be in fact negligible, and the last foundation for any doubt that the Scriptures have come down to us substantially as they were written has now been removed. Both the *authenticity* and the general *integrity* of the books of the New Testament may be regarded as finally established." '

IV. THE INNER WITNESS OF THE SPIRIT

The matter, however, does not rest upon the above internal and external evidences, at least so far as the truly Christian theologian is concerned. The Church itself has always claimed that, though it has a special duty carefully to preserve and carefully to hand down the records which God has given to it, yet God Himself is also concerned in this process. The Christian can discern a special and unique quality in the books of Holy Scripture. There is something about their contents which accords with the claim that the Holy Spirit is the primary author of all Holy Scripture. In other words, it accepts the Bible on the grounds of the *testimonium internum Sancti Spiritus*—i.e. an inward witness of the Spirit in the believing reader's heart which accords with the claims made concerning its authority in the text of Scripture itself. To put the matter in another way, the Church did not create the Canon of the New Testament. On the contrary, it has been mainly the Canon of Scripture which (under the power of the Holy Spirit) has been responsible for bringing the Church itself into being. But once having awakened to the voice of God, the Church is able to recognize in Holy Scripture the divine instrument which the Holy Spirit continually uses in completing God's work of the 'new creation' amongst men. In the last analysis there is a sense in which the Canon is self-authenticating, in much the same way (though *He* was *sui generis*) that our Lord Himself was the bearer of His own credentials. That this was intended to be the case is supported by a considerable body of internal evidence in the books of Holy Scripture themselves.

Our Lord Himself described one of the characteristics of His people, as follows: 'A stranger will they not follow, but will flee from him: for they know not the voice of strangers. . . .? My sheep hear my voice, and I know them, and they follow me' (Jn. x. 5, 27). This was to be one result of the promised presence of the Holy Spirit in the Church, as is further explained in such Scriptures as Jn. xvi. 13, 14, and 1 Cor. ii. 14, 16. Perhaps, John has stated this matter in the boldest form in his first Epistle, where much of his argument is dependent upon the effects amongst the believing people of the 'anointing from the Holy One' which enables them to 'know' and to discern (1 Jn. ii. 20, *et seq.*) what is 'of' or 'from' God and what is not from God. It is on this principle that the Church finally bases its conviction that Holy Scripture is indeed the Word of God. The external evidence can bring us only to what some older theologians have called 'historical faith'. It is the Holy Spirit, working in and through Scripture, which brings us to full Christian 'faith', 'spiritual apprehension' or 'conviction'.

In classic passages of the *Institutes of the Christian Religion*, Calvin refers to this important matter in the following words:

'There has very generally prevailed a most pernicious error, that the Scriptures have only so much weight as is conceded to them by the suffrages of the Church; as though the eternal and inviolable truth of God depended on the arbitrary will of men' (I. vii. 1). 'If the Christian Church has been from the beginning founded on the writings of the prophets and the preaching of the apostles, wherever that doctrine is found, the approbation of it has certainly preceded the formation of the Church; since without it the Church itself had never existed' (I. vii. 2). 'It must be maintained . . . that we are not established in the belief of the doctrine till we are indubitably persuaded that God is its Author. The principal proof, therefore, of the Scriptures is everywhere derived from the character of the divine speaker' (I. vii. 4). 'The Scripture will . . . only be effectual to produce the saving knowledge of God, when the certainty of it shall be founded on the internal persuasion of the Holy Spirit' (I. viii. 13).

VI. THE ESSENTIAL GROUNDS FOR THE ACCEPTANCE

In a valuable study of the Canon of Scripture, entitled *The Authority of the New Testament*, Professor N. B. Stonehouse[1] emphasizes repeatedly that this whole problem must be frankly considered in the light of the Christian philosophy of history and the total Christian view of God and the world. To quote a relevant passage: 'It is our conclusion that the idea of canonicity has meaning and validity only if Christian theism, the theism of the Bible, is true. Implicit in the idea of a divinely authoritative Scripture is the thought of God as self-existent and self-sufficient, the Creator and Ruler of the universe . . . it was necessary that God should reveal Himself directly in history by word and deed. That special and direct revelation in history, which found its centre and goal in the history of Jesus Christ, possesses an objective, final character, of permanent validity and significance for men. The inscripturation of that revelation through the agency of the Holy Spirit was due precisely to the need that a permanent and trustworthy record should be pro-

[1] Published as a section of *The Infallible Word*, a symposium by the members of the Faculty of the Westminster Theological Seminary, Philadelphia.

vided of the fact and the meaning of the divine action in history' (p. 95).

The position might be briefly outlined as follows. The Christian sees that God, who is above and over all the course of history, has intervened in the affairs of men through Israel and, at length, decisively in the person of Jesus the Messiah. In accepting Him as the Son of God, the Christian accepts the Old Testament with all its implications, and there naturally follows an acceptance of the completed records of God's revelation, which is found in the New Testament. 'The only one who speaks in the New Testament with an authority that is underived and self-authenticating is the Lord.' The divine Messiahship of Jesus is then the basic fact behind the formation of the New Testament. 'The apostolic authority which speaks forth in the New Testament is never detached from the authority of the Lord' and it is 'the apostles who constituted the link between the Lord Himself and the Scriptures of the New Testament' (pp. 109–114).

The various documents which came into being after the earthly life of our Lord are essentially further unfoldings of the nature and meaning of His words and deeds. In the final analysis, the Christian case for the Canon rests squarely on a basic conviction. It is that, in the context of the Being of God and of His revelation of Himself in Christ (mediated to us through patriarch, prophet and apostle) we possess in Holy Scripture a body of divinely authoritative and self-authenticating documents.

CHAPTER SIX

OUR LORD'S BIBLE

HE who desires to live in the spirit of the New Testament must make it his aim to find and to follow the mind of Christ. It is a flagrant misnomer for a man to call himself a true Christian and then to decline obedience to what is clearly Christ's teaching on any given matter. Our Lord Himself asked, "Why call ye me, Lord, Lord, and do not the things which I say?' (Lk. vi. 46). The candid reader of the Gospels will surely be impressed by the fact that the outlook of the apostles has been dominated and wholly transformed by One greater than they. The impact of His Person upon their thought-life has been faithfully recorded in the Gospels and elsewhere in the New Testament. As true disciples, it is incumbent upon us not to attempt to 'edit' our Master's words in any respect, and His attitude to the Old Testament must be included.

I. A KEY REFERENCE

The statement in which our Lord's view of the Old Testament is seen at its clearest is found in Jn. x. 34. At a crucial moment in the midst of a very threatening situation, He bases the whole of His argument on *one word* in Ps. lxxxii. But the significant point is the description which He gives of His source of authority. The Jews had already taken up stones to stone Him to death because they contended that in His explanation of the parable of the Good Shepherd He has 'blasphemed', since He (in their view, being only the son of a carpenter) had described Himself as equal with God. Our Lord replied: 'Is it not written in your law, I said, Ye are gods? If he called them gods, unto whom the word of God came (and the scripture cannot be broken), say ye of him, whom the Father sanctified and sent into the world, Thou blasphemest; because I said, I am the Son of God?' (Jn. x. 34–36). Two points in this reply call for special notice, first that He collectively refers to Scripture as 'the law'—i.e. the whole of the Old Testament is regarded as binding on His hearers, and second that He adds (with marked emphasis) 'and the scripture cannot be broken'. Exegetical scholars have pointed out that the Greek equivalent used for our word 'broken' is the same as that which is employed for breaking the sabbath (cf. also Mt. v. 19). The whole force of His reply to His critics rests on the grounds that 'the scripture cannot be broken'. As Professor B. B. Warfield has commented on this passage, it is 'the strongest possible assertion of the indefectible authority of Scripture'.

The most striking means through which to study how our Lord uses Old Testament Scripture is to read through one of the Synoptic Gospels (e.g. Matthew's) and, then, through John's Gospel, making a careful list of each of His references to 'the law' or to 'the scriptures'.[1] An appeal is made at one time or another to almost every main section of the Old Testament. The bare list of quotations is, to say the least, impressive. There are examples of almost every type of citation. Of the practical uses to which our Lord put Old Testament Scripture the best-known examples are those which reveal His method of repelling the temptations in the wilderness. In each case, He opposed to the subtle inducements employed by the tempter a simple 'It is written'. With this may be compared His replies to His critics, 'Is it not for this cause that ye err, that ye know not the scriptures, nor the power of God?' (Mk. xii. 24).

II. TWO MAIN TRENDS IN OUR LORD'S REFERENCES

For the purposes of the present chapter, however, we are chiefly interested to show how our Lord's use of Scripture demonstrates two important principles in His own thought-life. First, the words of Scripture are quoted as *the very words of God*. For example, what appears in the text of the Old Testament simply as a comment on the creation of woman (Gn. ii. 24) is quoted in the first Gospel as 'He which made them . . . said, For this cause shall a man leave his father and mother' (Mt. xix. 4, 5). Secondly, the explanation which our Lord repeatedly gives of certain strange or threatening happenings in His life and of His

[1] See Appendix I (page 132) for a list of the most important references.

E

expectations for the future is simply 'that the scriptures might be fulfilled.' For example, 'I was daily with you in the temple teaching, and ye took me not: but this is done that the scriptures might be fulfilled' (Mk. xiv. 49, and cf. Jn. xiii. 18). Again, 'Then saith Jesus unto them, All ye shall be offended in me this night: for it is written, I will smite the shepherd, and the sheep of the flock shall be scattered abroad' (Mt. xxvi. 31).

The pages of the Gospels are punctuated by such references of the Old Testament to the happenings in the life of Christ. They are mostly introduced to us in His own words. They afford the most graphic possible evidence that He was publicly applying to Himself in detail the messianic prophecies.

III. THE EXTENT OF OUR LORD'S KNOWLEDGE

It has not been overlooked that some readers will question this method of taking the internal evidences from the Gospels in order to demonstrate from them our Lord's attitude to the Old Testament, and then to deduce from them that this should also be the attitude of the Christian in the twentieth century. They will, no doubt, object that 'Our Lord was the child of His time,' or that He 'simply shared the limited or mistaken outlook of the Jews of His time.' Some will, no doubt suggest that, when He 'emptied Himself' of the divine majesty and took upon Himself the 'form of a servant' (Phil. ii. 7), during this period He did not retain the type of knowledge which is essentially divine. They would hold that He 'voluntarily limited Himself so that on earth He was unable to see "beyond the errors" of His Jewish teachers and associates.' In reply, all that need be said is that such suggestions are in plain defiance of the internal evidence.

Though, from one point of view, our Lord was truly human and was possessed of a truly human mind and outlook, at the same time the New Testament does not lead us to believe that He surrendered His divine consciousness. There are numerous allusions to a knowledge which was beyond the recognized normal human capacities, e.g. the doctors in the temple confronted by a twelve-year-old son of a village carpenter 'were amazed at his understanding and his answers' (Lk. ii. 47), and, on a second occasion, 'marvelled, saying, How knoweth this man letters, having never learned?' (Jn. vii. 15). Similarly, when an early disciple, Nathanael, asked the Lord how He had such an intimate knowledge of him, who was hitherto unknown, he received the reply: 'Before Philip called thee, when thou wast under the fig tree, I saw thee' (Jn. i. 48). The fact is that, if the evidence of the Gospel writers is accepted, our Lord was in possession throughout His lifetime of far more than 'the insights of a religious genius' or of extra-sensory perception for which historic or modern parallel can be adduced.

Again, whatever may earlier have been the case, there can be no possible ambiguity concerning our Lord's powers subsequent to resurrection. Yet it is precisely at this point that our Lord's references to the Old Testament take on a still further comprehensiveness. He rebukes two disciples who were distressed over the tragedy of His unexpected death, commenting 'O foolish men, and slow of heart to believe in all that the prophets have spoken! Behoved it not the Christ to suffer these things, and to enter into his glory? And beginning from Moses and from all the prophets, he interpreted to them in all the scriptures the things concerning himself' (Lk. xxiv. 25–27). Later, the same evening, He repeated this interpretative outline of the true meaning of the Old Testament to the eleven disciples and certain other disciples. It is plain that our Lord elevated the Old Testament to its highest pinnacle of interest and authority when He was clearly endowed with supernatural powers, subsequent to His resurrection and immediately prior to ascension. It is significant that once again at this time we have the familiar phrase 'It is written' (Lk. xxiv. 46). There is room for no shadow of doubt that—so far as His recorded words are concerned—our Lord expected His disciples to accept the full authority of the Old Testament.

There is a further consideration of great significance which meets us in this particular context. Our Lord was not simply vindicating the authority of the Old Testament but He was asserting that His own sufferings and subsequent glory were the main themes of the Old Testament. The long story of Israel going back into patriarchal times can only be truly understood when focused on to the central point of the message of the Bible —the fact and meaning of the death and resurrection of Christ.

IV. THE ATTITUDE OF THE APOSTLES

When we pass to consider the outlook in these matters of Paul and the other apostles, we notice a prevailing tendency throughout the rest of the New Testament, which reverently accepts the factual statements and the teaching of the Old Testament. There is no difference in this respect of reverent submission to the 'It is written' between any of the New Testament writers. They all speak of the 'Scriptures' as carrying with them the fullest divine authority. Paul and John imply that their own apostolic letters carry the authority of God and are to be implicitly obeyed as if they were the law of God. Similarly, when introducing an Old Testament citation on several occasions, they begin with the phrase 'God says' a sentence which (in the original context) is not presented by the Old Testament as being the words of God. An example of this is 1 Cor. vi. 16, 'The twain, saith he, shall become one flesh.'

But more important still, they frequently use 'Scripture says' interchangeably with 'God says'. On at least three occasions a statement made by the writer of a Psalm is quoted with the introduction 'the Holy Spirit saith "God said" ', whereas in the Old Testament context there is no such reference to God. For example, Heb. iii. 7 quotes Ps. xcv. 7, in the form 'Even as the Holy Ghost saith.' The disciples, in Acts iv. 25, cite Ps. ii. 1, as being God speaking 'by the Holy Ghost, by the mouth of our father David thy servant.' Again, Acts xiii. 34, in presenting the phrase 'He hath spoken on this wise, I will give you the holy and sure blessings of David', attributes Is. lv. 3 to a direct statement of God.

It is perhaps even more striking still to examine closely Paul's description of Old Testament Scripture in his discussion of the advantages which a Jew possesses when searching for salvation. He writes, 'First of all, that they (i.e. the Jews) were entrusted with the oracles of God,' and then proceeds to appeal to 'It is written . . .' The word 'oracle' is a strong word to use for the Old Testament unless he firmly believed that it was in fact the authoritative revelation of God. Again, it could not be made clearer that 'God' and 'Scripture' are used almost interchangeably by the apostles than by comparing Gal. iii. 8 with Rom. ix. 17. In the first instance Paul writes, 'The scripture, foreseeing that God would justify the Gentiles by faith, preached the gospel beforehand unto Abraham, saying, In thee shall all the nations be blessed,' when it is God who is recorded in the Old Testament as using these words. In the second instance, he states 'Scripture saith unto Pharaoh, For this very purpose did I raise thee up . . .' That is, 'Scripture saith' is equated with God speaking.

In some books of the New Testament, the writers express themselves as if they are thinking of God as the writer who is really addressing the reader. This is made very clear by the use of the present tense in the Epistle to the Hebrews: 'The Holy Ghost saith, Today if ye shall hear his voice' (Heb. iii. 7). A large section of Hebrews i is taken up by four quotations (each selected from a different Psalm) and all of them are introduced as 'He said' (i.e. God said) whereas in the original Old Testament context God does not necessarily appear to be the speaker. In two of the Psalms, quoted as if God is speaking, He seems in the original context to be the One to whom the psalmist is speaking.

Such a method of quotation does not at all accord with the outlook of modern scholarship ! But its usage is accounted for in the New Testament by the overwhelming sense of the writers that it is God who is the primary speaker, or author, in the Old Testament.

V. AN IMPORTANT EXAMPLE

Perhaps the most significant in this connection of all Old Testament quotations in the New Testament is that of Paul in Gal. iii. 16. He is speaking of God's purpose to reconcile the nations on the basis of faith in His Son. The work of the latter was the true fulfilment of the promise to Abraham that in Him should 'all the nations be blessed.' He is wishing to emphasize that all the promises had received their fulfilment in the coming and the work of Christ. He continues, 'Now to Abraham were the promises spoken, and to his seed. He saith not, And to seeds, as of many; but as of one, And to thy seed, which is Christ.' If

Paul had been arguing in present-day non-rabbinical style he would have said: 'It is noteworthy that the Scripture uses a word which can refer to a single descendant and not one which could denote only a plurality of descendants'. The inference is that the details of the Old Testament, in Paul's view, are to be relied upon. The human writer is of importance only so far as the Holy Spirit uses him. For the apostles, the Scriptures of the Old Testament were the products of a human writer who was under the power and control of God's Spirit (2 Pet. i. 21), or, conversely, they are words which the Spirit has chosen to say by the mouth of a human author (Acts i. 16 and iv. 25). It is because of their divine origin and because the voice of God is heard in the Holy Scriptures that they must become the court of appeal in matters of faith and conduct.

VI. THE APOSTLES' VIEW OF THEIR OWN WRITINGS

Such an attitude as described above is not confined to the claims for the Old Testament. It is also applied to the New Testament. For example, it is instructive to study Paul's use of the authority which had been given to him as an apostle. He demands the same respect for his own apostolic writings to the churches as he has enforced for the Law and the Prophets. In 2 Thes. ii. 15, he does not hesitate to state 'so then, brethren, stand fast, and hold the traditions which ye were taught, whether by word, or by epistle of ours'; in 2 Thes. iii. 6, 'withdraw yourselves from every brother that walketh disorderly, and not after the tradition which they received of us'; and in iii. 14 of the same book he adds, 'And if any man obeyeth not our word by this epistle, note that man, that ye have no company with him, to the end that he may be ashamed.' The implications are clear. John puts the same view positively when he describes the blessedness which will come to those who pay careful attention to the Revelation: 'Blessed is he that readeth, and they that hear the words of the prophecy, and keep the things which are written therein: for the time is at hand' (Rev. i. 3); compare also Rev. xxii. 7. He concludes, however, with the warnings in xxii. 18, 19, that 'If any man shall add unto them, God shall add unto him the plagues which are written in this book: and if any man shall take away from the words of the book of this prophecy, God shall take away his part from the tree of life.'

VII. A RECENT STUDY

There has recently appeared a study by Professor C. H. Dodd of the Old Testament as used by New Testament writers.[1] Approaching from a very different viewpoint and with a different purpose from that of the present writer, a number of the conclusions set out by the lecturer afford support at several points to what has been written above. How may we account for the unanimity with which the apostles proclaimed their teaching concerning Jesus the Messiah? The lecturer replies, 'The impression that we derive from examination of such applications of the Old Testament Scripture to the events of the *kerygma* (i.e. 'the proclamation' of the gospel) by the New Testament theologians is that they are working upon certain accepted assumptions.'

The final conclusions which Professor C. H. Dodd draws from examination of the data are:

1. The way the New Testament writers quote the Old Testament passages is not accounted for simply by the possession of some primitive anthology of messianic proof-texts, but indicates an attitude and a certain method of biblical study, which was used by the apostles and early Christian teachers.

2. This method included: (i) the selection of large sections of the Old Testament particularly from Isaiah, Jeremiah, certain Minor Prophets and the Psalms; (ii) the understanding of these fundamental passages as whole and 'in their total context', and it is the latter which controls the basis of their whole argument; and (iii) the understanding of all the relevant Scriptures upon certain consistent principles of interpretation, which kept in view 'the determinate counsel of God', which has been fulfilled in the facts of the gospel and which determined for the apostles the meaning of these facts.

[1] Given as a series of Stone Lectures in March 1950 in Princeton Theological Seminary, it has now been published under the title of *According to the Scriptures* (Nisbet, 1952).

3. 'This whole body of material—the passages of Old Testament Scripture with their application to the Gospel facts—is common to all the main portions of the New Testament, and in particular it provided the starting point for the theological distinctions of Paul, the author of the Epistle to the Hebrews, and the fourth evangelist.'

Professor Dodd adds (p. 133) 'the main line of interpretation of the Old Testament exemplified in the New is not only consistent and intelligent in itself, but is also founded upon a genuinely historical understanding of the process of the religious —I should prefer to say the prophetic—history of Israel as a whole.'

CHAPTER SEVEN

DIFFICULTIES FROM SCHOLARSHIP AND THE SCIENCES

THE Bible has from early times been ruthlessly criticized by those who do not accept this Book for what it claims to be. Particularly during the last hundred years the Bible's statements have been carefully scrutinized and a lowered place accorded to them in the sum of modern knowledge. It is, therefore, important that—as far as space permits—we should examine the general nature of the criticisms which have been brought against these documents and assess their validity. In subsequent chapters some of the major difficulties will be considered in greater detail.

The criticisms have come mainly along two lines of modern research. In the first place there has been the impact of modern scholarship—whether linguistic, literary, textual, or historical— and, with the latter, must also be included research in archaeology. As well as criticism, each of these branches of study has also brought its valuable quota of new knowledge to the understanding of the Bible. In the main it has been an unbalanced application of hypothesis and theory within a section of these studies which has brought opposition to the statements of the Bible books. In the second place, a hundred years of development in the natural sciences has brought about almost a totally new approach to the problem of the origin of life and cosmogony as a whole. The workers in all of these fields have, not unnaturally, claimed (because of the spiritual content of the Bible, and because of the high claims of its writers) that they feel entitled to expect a certain accuracy of detail when the statements of Scripture impinge upon their branches of knowledge. They require that at those points where they are able to subject it to the appropriate tests in their own particular department they should be free to do so. Scholars, scientists and other workers of all kinds have therefore not hesitated to subject the books of Holy Scripture to a most thorough scrutiny from their point of view. In some cases, their zeal has exceeded the bounds which are legitimate within the methodology of their own branches of science and has resulted in demands being made of the Bible which could scarcely be expected of any ancient document. It is certain that no other comparable body of literature, not even the Classics, has received such thorough critical attention! In the result, the Bible has compelled a new respect from its critics.

Certain general comments are relevant at this point. In the early days of such work, some scholarly and scientific extremists made claims which further and more recent work has greatly modified. Also, it cannot be emphasized sufficiently that the aim of the Bible is not to provide a literary masterpiece, a manual of ancient world history or a text-book of science. It was brought into being primarily to provide an authoritative, because God-given, 'history of redemption,' and in particular, to present Christ as the Revealer of God and Saviour of men. It tells of God's continual intervention to save men, of the final revealing and redeeming action of God in Christ.

It should not be expected of the Bible that it will provide a detailed scientific account, in modern terms, of the world's origin and of its constitution. On the other hand, it must surely be given due weight that the order of events which the book of Genesis gives for the origin of the major forms of life, compared with that derived from palaeontology, presents striking similarities, to say the least! When it is remembered that, so far as is known, no comparable study to that of modern geology and related sciences was practised in Egypt, Palestine or Babylonia during the times when the book of Genesis was recorded, its freedom from the superstitions and gross mistakes of other ancient literature is remarkable. The residuum of assured scientific results, which appear to be incompatible with plain biblical statement, appears to be meagre in the extreme. When one pauses to recall that the Bible's library of sixty-six books was written over a period of 1,500 years, and by some forty different men who were of all types of ordinary education or of none, and that few of them wrote in the same immediate vicinity as each other, the degree of unanimity and accuracy which has been attained is nothing short of a miracle.

I. SCHOLARSHIP

Let us, then, briefly consider the methods, apparatus and available knowledge which an accurate scholar is able to bring to a study of the Old Testament. In the first place we must notice that strict scholarship is essentially negative in its methodology and application. Scholarship cannot be actively constructive, for it is not entitled to add to the materials or data which it undertakes to examine. In the case of an ancient document its function is simply to scrutinize it, to compare it with other findings which are already believed to be assured on sufficient available evidence, to assess its validity, and to integrate the findings with the present assured results and available knowledge. It is not a function of truly scientific scholarship to offer, at least in its own name (and, particularly, from inadequate evidence), conjectural emendations to fill the gaps in the document or to put forward hypotheses which are based on such conjectural 'evidence'. If such conjectures are offered they must be plainly indicated to be the writer's own reconstructions and kept in a strictly secondary position, however plausible the results of speculation may seem. Later unsuspecting readers of a commentary or text-book ought not to be offered in the name of scholarship what is simply the result of subjective speculation, however 'scholarly' the writer otherwise may be. The best linguistic scholars have in general not offended in this way, but some of their lesser disciples have tended to do so. It is in this area that a great deal of the supposed conflict between scholarship and the Bible will be found to have originated.

That the above is not nearly so academic as it might seem will more readily be appreciated when it is added that much of the criticism of the Old Testament does not come under the heading of true linguistic or historical scholarship at all. It ought to be far more widely known than it is, especially to the younger theological students, that many of the more popular books critical of the Old Testament (published between the years 1890 and 1930, or even later) include an assortment of the true findings of the best scholarship compounded with an extensive amount of conjecture. Old Testament scholarship has only comparatively recently reacted against the older extremism.

The following consideration will illustrate the ease with which conjecture may replace a valid judgment. Some of the writers, and editors, of the older text-books of the Old Testament often assert that a given word reveals an 'early' linguistic form, or another a 'late' form. Similarly, one section may be designated as 'early' in style and another as 'late'. But the writer is here very frequently exceeding the bounds of objective scholarship simply because in many instances there are not the available data on which such comparisons can be accurately made. What he should say is: 'I feel on subjective grounds' or 'the impression made on my mind is that this is early,' or 'this is late.' But that is a very different matter and must not necessarily be regarded as a result of true scholarship. It is based on subjective criteria and may be little more than a guess. There is no body of contemporary Hebrew literature with which the various stages of 'classical' Hebrew literature may be checked. Indeed, it is not until a comparatively late date and, in the main, not much anterior to the time of our Lord, that other Hebrew literature becomes available on the basis of which such comparisons can be truly effected. Yet a good deal of the conflict has raged around the words 'early' and 'late'.

II. LITERARY CRITICISM OF THE OLD TESTAMENT

Similar methods were extended to the related historical fields. For example, the 'Graf-Wellhausen' hypothesis of the compilation of the Pentateuch gave rise to the immense amount of conjecture concerning not only the origin of the Pentateuch but also other later parts of the Old Testament. Such conjecture naturally exerted a considerable influence on subsequent historical studies of the national development of Israel. Yet, on close examination the whole body of thought which, somewhat gratuitously, attributes the authorship of the greater part of the Pentateuch to later compilers and 'editors' (who are said to have put their words into the mouth of Moses) is found to be suspended on very tenuous threads of evidence. The important point, however, for our purpose here is to point out that assuming the very thing which had to be proved (i.e. the correctness of the 'Graf-Wellhausen' hypothesis), many writers working on the later history of Israel have treated the documentary hypotheses concerning the origin of the Pentateuch as 'axiomatic' for much of their further work. In other words, many of the objections which are advanced against the Old Testament and concerning the Bible's own account of Israel's history are as true, or as false, as the 'Graf-Wellhausen' hypothesis. Scholarship has become increasingly impressed with the unsatisfactory nature of this hypothesis. It will be interesting to see what will take its place and what will be the results for other sections of Old Testament study.

III. ARCHAEOLOGY

Archaeology, having on the whole a lighter task than linguistic scholarship because much of its data is more easily handled and compared, has had a good deal to say concerning the facts of biblical history. At some stages, certain of the earliest findings in Palestine, Egypt, Mesopotamia and Asia Minor appeared to conflict at several crucial points with biblical history. Some of the recent work has added its quota of new criticisms of the Old Testament and raised further difficulties in relation to other sections of the Book. In the main, however, archaeological study has cast a flood of light upon the contemporary backgrounds of many of the books of the Bible, and has thrown into bolder relief the history of Israel as recorded in the Old and New Testaments. Recent discovery has gone a long way to confirm at almost every point where it can clearly be tested the accuracy of the facts as presented in Bible history. Archaeology has also served to compel modification of a number of the more extreme hypotheses of some of the earlier critical commentators on the Old Testament. More of these conjectures should have been abandoned, or modified, than so far have actually received such correction. To put it at its very lowest, the result of over a hundred years of archaeological research in the Near East has been to go far towards vindicating the claims of Bible history.

IV. PHILOSOPHY OF RELIGION

Perhaps, however, the chief culprit in the earlier series of misplaced criticisms of the Bible was neither linguistic scholarship nor archaeology, but the philosophy of religion. It has been the fashion in this branch of study to work with bold conjectures. For example, the student of the Old Testament historical statements, such as the reference in Genesis to the stone on which Jacob slept at Bethel, has sometimes been furnished with a 'scholarly' note in which it is confidently asserted that here could be traced the influence of folk-lore and of other ancient religions. It has been further suggested that the stone was 'obviously' something which indicated the influence of 'stone-worship', or it was simply a 'totem'. Others have suggested that Jacob's imagination, quickened in the unusual circumstances, conjured up for him a supposed vision of angels at Bethel, and later, at Peniel, a seeming vision of God! Whatever else such a commentating may be it is not scholarship, nor is it science. It is an example of pure imagination and of the substitution of plausible conjecture for conservative and scientific research.

Unfortunately, such assumptions soon come to be regarded as fundamental principles. For example, it is an axiom with many philosophers of religion that Israel evolved its monotheism from an original polytheism. They have then proceeded to interpret various stages of Israel's history in the light of their original assumption. The conflict, therefore, between the philosopher of religion and the Bible's assertion of an original monotheism clearly arises from a sweeping speculation and not from ascertained scientific data. The fact is that, though at present it has been largely ignored, there is a good deal of evidence for the opposite contention that mankind at large lapsed from an original monotheism into a series of polytheisms.

V. THE NATURAL SCIENCES

There is, however, another large group of research workers, the natural scientists, among whom the geologist and biologist have most come into conflict with the Old Testament. Yet here it is chiefly only with the opening chapters of Genesis (i.e. with the cosmology of the Bible) that they have been disposed to quarrel. At first sight an interpretation, based upon an accurate exegesis of the first three chapters of the Bible, might appear to be at variance at certain points with the findings of modern science.

Deeper acquaintance, however, will compel the careful worker to decline hasty judgment and to reassess both sets of data. He will discover that there is a basic coherence between them and that they may be related as a glove is to the hand. In any case, in the natural sciences, as elsewhere, the Christian man must be the foremost in wanting to know the truth as far as research can achieve it. The Bible itself encourages such research when it emphasizes the ultimate importance and beneficence of truth.

Yet, here again, it must be claimed that we shall be allowed to scrutinize the assumptions and methodology with which the scientist proposes to operate. The scientist himself is often surprisingly unaware that his procedures and reasoning are not necessarily universally valid in all the other fields of study. Even within his own branch he pays far too little attention to the requirements of philosophy or logic. His empirical methods tend to be taken over uncritically from his predecessors, and because they seem to work in a limited sphere, he may see no reason for scrutiny of his basic assumptions.[1] He also constantly tends to assume that his findings in one segment of research will necessarily apply in another. But it is a big step to conclude from the experience of the present time and its practical results that the same relations, laws, speeds of reaction, and other factors were necessarily operating in the same manner at the beginning of time. In fact, the question of origins will probably long need to remain an open question. The scientist is compelled to enter the realm of hypothesis and unproved assertion the moment he leaves his immediate field and attempts to pronounce upon such problems as those of origin, or to give a reason why things should be as they actually are. It is quite legitimate for him, or anyone else, to speculate, so long as it is understood that the results are not necessarily scientific 'fact'.

VI. FAULTS ON BOTH SIDES

On both sides there have been too facile assumptions con-

[1] A very searching—it might be claimed a devastating—examination of the modern scientist's disregard of the necessity for self-scrutiny will be found in *Science is a Sacred Cow*, by Anthony Standen (Dutton, N.Y., 1950).

cerning what the Bible does, and does not say, and on both sides there has been far too great a preoccupation with speculative reconstruction rather than with the true findings of biblical scholarship and of science. Between a careful interpretation of the Bible, i.e. one in which the Book is allowed to speak in its own language and is interpreted in conformity with its own nature, and, on the other hand, the strict and confirmed findings of science, the area of divergence is virtually negligible.

It is true that there remains a small residuum where the present interpretations of science do appear to be at variance with some sections of Bible interpretation. It is, however, by no means settled that the Bible is wrong! The remarks above have not been prompted by the view that the Christian needs the confirmation of science for his faith, or needs to be over-anxious concerning reconciling new research with the biblical data. Our object in glancing at science is simply to emphasize that the scientist, as much as anyone else, must be prepared for self-examination and the continual discipline of ensuring that his findings are valid. Since knowledge today is moving forward at such a rapid pace, it is unlikely that it will be possible to settle for some time to come what the exact position is in the areas of conflict between science and religion. But one fact already clearly stands out. When comparisons are attempted between modern discovery and the 'science' of other ancient documents, on the one hand, and with the biblical documents on the other, it remains a matter for astonishment that the contemporary superstitions of earlier history and the scientific 'mistakes' in other literatures are noticeably absent from the Bible. Not only so, but a number of incidental observations in the Bible, e.g. concerning disease, which at first were too speedily acclaimed by opponents as being 'mistakes', have subsequently been found to be accurate observations. They have also revealed an accord with accredited modern scientific views for which it is difficult to account apart from the claims of the Bible that its thought world has been derived from a supernatural source, which itself is in causal relation with the physical world as we find it.

It is a fact to be deplored that there should have been such unhappy relationships and so many unnecessary conflicts between the leaders of the Christian Church and scientists. Both the defender of the Bible and also the scientist should have adhered more carefully to their own strictly limited spheres of study. The basic conflict has been, and still is, between the Bible and various forms of materialistic and speculative philosophy. There is no means for resolving this conflict so long as the materialistic philosopher persists in excluding from his thought world what he is pleased to call the 'God-hypothesis'.

CHAPTER EIGHT

DIFFICULTIES IN THE OLD TESTAMENT

CONDITIONED as he is by modern critical and scientific attitudes, even the best disposed reader is today perplexed by some features of the Old Testament. He comes to it with his mind already deeply influenced by certain popular misconceptions. He has gained the impression that scholarship and science have rendered it impossible to accept much of the Old Testament at its face value. Indeed, the more sweeping generalizations of some critical scholars have tended to suggest that little credence can be given to the opening books of the Bible in so far as they claim to be a record of true history. Also, it is suggested that the last series of books in the Old Testament, usually described as 'prophetic,' are to be regarded as being more in the nature of rousing expository sermons to the nation than as true predictions of future events.

To notice all the many smaller difficulties raised by this type of approach would require a large volume. For our present purpose, it will be sufficient to classify them and to consider several typical cases. During the late nineteenth century roughly six main lines of criticism of the Old Testament emerged:

1. Criticism of the early *history* of Israel, as advanced in the Old Testament.

2. Criticism of the account of the *religion* of Israel as recorded in the Old Testament.

3. *Literary* criticism of the documents (chiefly of the first five books, the Psalms and Isaiah).

4. *Archaeological* criticism of certain details, e.g. in the historical books and Daniel.

5. Criticism of the accounts of the *miracles* and predictive *prophecy*.

6. *Moral* criticism of Israel's actions, arising from God's commands to the nation.

I. CRITICISM OF THE HISTORY

In recent years there has been on the part of most workers in this field an increasing tendency to adopt a more conservative attitude. In the minds of many of the older critics, however, there lies at the back of all the other problems, such as those of the authorship and validity of the documents, a fundamental suspicion of history as it is recorded in the Old Testament. This is particularly true of its opening books. It would not be far wrong to affirm that some critics came to the early parts of the Old Testament already expecting the book of Genesis to be composed of a series of legends, 'sagas' and 'myths', which have been worked up by later hands. The exodus from Egypt and Israel's wanderings in the wilderness are in part regarded as pseudo-history, embroidered by later patriots, on the return from the exile in Babylon, in order to provide a satisfactory introduction to the nation's history. Scholars appear so far to have been slow in accepting what is undoubtedly contemporary historical literature now available which indicates that the early chapters of Genesis should not be lightly regarded as unhistorical. Later criticisms of some sections of the historical and poetical books tend to base themselves on the reconstructions of the background for the first five or six books—assuming the truth of these reconstructions.

The story of Israel is in this way conformed to the usual pattern in which later patriotic writers enshrine the surviving stories of the migrations of any other nomadic tribe. Israel is regarded as making its way westwards, led by legendary heroes, from the valley of the Euphrates into eastern Egypt and then subsequently in a north-easterly direction into Palestine. Here, after various wars of conquest and much civil strife, it achieved some degree of inner unity and emerged into what may be regarded as something approaching true history.

The importance of such an attitude of modern criticism for those who are devotees of the Bible is that the latter are compelled to face a serious question. If the claims of the first five books cannot be taken at their face value, and are not to be regarded as true history, and if they were mostly compiled at a late date, then the claim to divine origin for the theology of

Israel becomes reduced to being the modified 'divinity' of the special genius for religion revealed by Israel's lawgivers and prophets. A God-given objective revelation is replaced by the subjective 'insights' of her prophets. Certain basic doctrines which furnish the foundations for the theology of the New Testament are thus seriously undermined or attenuated.

Some of these biblical doctrines, taking their rise from Genesis and Exodus, ought briefly to be noticed. The Genesis account of the origin of all things through a freely chosen act or series of acts on the part of the one true God would no longer furnish the fundamental explanation of the world and life as we know it. The account of man's origin through a direct intervention of God imparting to him a spirit, self-consciousness and intellectual powers much in advance of the 'highest' animal would need to be deducted from the doctrine of man. The Ten Commandments, the ceremonial law and the moral law of Exodus would be demoted from their authority as divine commands supernaturally communicated to Moses. They would become late codifications of Israel's 'common law' in the time of Ezra. There is a world of difference between proposing to oneself obedience to the Ten Commandments because 'God spake all these words, saying . . .' (Ex. xx. 1) and the incorporating of them into our thought life as useful maxims borrowed from a nation which has shown the greatest genius for religion.

It must then be asked: 'Are we compelled by the valid objective findings of the best historical scholarship to modify our views of the claim of the first five books of the Bible? Has historical research revealed that these and later books are unhistorical or inaccurate?' The correct answer would appear to be that, while certainly no one knows enough or can check sufficient references by valid evidence to prove that these Old Testament books are true, up to the present no one has possessed either sufficient knowledge or data to demonstrate the untruthfulness of these books. Where it has been possible to test them by clear historical evidence the documents have emerged, apart from a few scribal errors, surprisingly unscathed. At points where earlier historical and archaeological research had appeared to conflict, later discovery has gone far to demonstrate the essential accuracy of the Old Testament records as history. 'A few swallows do not make a summer.' Yet it is worth remarking that the honourable emergence from criticism of the patriarchal period, of the historical books, of aberrant spellings of personal and place names, and also of details concerning kings and battles, has compelled a wholesome caution in those disposed to correct the Old Testament.

The older methods, with their marked tendency to approach the Bible documents with a preconceived evolutionary or Hegelian view of history, led inevitably to the imposition on the documents of a theoretical framework from which the biblical records were not permitted to stray on pain of emendation and hypothetical reconstruction. A more cautious mood and more conservative methods are evident today. This may be clearly seen from one of the most recent surveys of the results of research of the past thirty years: *The Old Testament and Modern Study*, being essays by members of the Society for Old Testament Studies, edited by H. H. Rowley (O.U.P.). Professor Rowley's introductory study, 'Trends in Old Testament Study' and Professor W. F. Albright's two chapters on 'The Old Testament and the Archaeology of Palestine and the Near East' have clearly indicated where many of the earlier hypotheses need to be corrected. In Professor Albright's section are found numerous references such as the following: 'Many biblical scholars of today seem to think that the situation has not changed since 1909 or 1919. They are sadly mistaken, and their error is now handicapping the progress of Old Testament research by perpetuating innumerable hypotheses and assumptions which cannot stand for a minute in the light of contemporary archaeology' (p. 2); and 'The tremendous significance of the new finds for the Bible can be realized in part by listing a few of the outstanding achievements of the spade: the revival of the Patriarchal Age through the excavations at Nuzu and Mari; the flood of light on Hebrew poetry and language as a result of the excavation of Ugarit; the vivid illumination of the beginnings of Mosaic legislation through the publication of Hittite and Assyrian, Sumerian and Eshnunna codes; new light on the Persian period of Jewish history from Egypt and Iran. But again it must be emphasized

that the really great contribution of ancient Eastern archaeology
has been in the total picture, which enables us to see the life of
the chosen people against the background of the surrounding
world. *This is a contribution before which everything else must fade
into insignificance.'*

One further point with regard to Old Testament history calls
for mention. Most of the early critics ignored or failed to take
sufficient account of the underlying suggestions of a 'plan' or
'purpose', which is so marked a feature of Old Testament history.
The modern historian may retort that he is unable to concede
any 'supernatural' plan; his scientific method allows him to take
notice of nothing but the recorded or documentary evidence.
He may object that the Christian is reading the evidence through
the 'tinted glasses' of his own 'supernaturalistic presuppositions'
concerning the providence of God. It is perhaps this clash of
views which throws into clearest relief the two worlds which
cannot be reconciled. The one world is that whose history is
conceived on such atheistic (or agnostic) presuppositions that it
cannot brook any suggestions of a supernatural plan at the back
of the history of any nation; it knows only the concept of the
evolutionary struggle from the simple to the complex which
has been borrowed from the natural sciences. The other world
accepts the 'teleological principle',[1] which operates from the
starting point that the world was brought into being by the one
true God and that His purpose has been and is being worked out
through 'the chosen people' (the Israel of the Old Testament)
and the Church (the Israel of the New Testament). At least this
much can fairly be claimed by the unbiased reader of the Bible
(though the non-Christian historian may not have eyes to see it);
the whole library of the sixty-six books, in spite of their diversity
of authorships and multiple sites of origin, are found to be
woven together into an impressive unity by the single thread of
God's plan and purpose in history.

II. CRITICISM OF THE RELIGION OF ISRAEL

Again, in approaching the earlier developments of the religion

---

[1] The term 'teleology' describes the study of the final 'purpose' or 'goal'
to which any movement tends. (Greek *telos*, meaning an 'end' or 'purpose'.)

of the Old Testament, some critics confront us with what are basically a series of plausible conjectures. Their evolutionary approach inhibits those scholars who are chiefly interested in the philosophy of religion from anticipating *a priori* that God could have, and admitting *a posteriori* that He had, instituted a monotheism from the beginning and preserved it in faithful patriarchal families and, later, in early Israel. They are more familiar with a 'God' who exercises only a very remote control. They are more at home with the deists.[1] The God of the Old Testament, however, is a Being who is very actively interested and purposefully intervening in the affairs of men.

Some writers seem content to see little more in the religious details of the patriarchal period and history of early Israel than traces of surviving shrines, ancestor-worship, animism, fetishes, stone-worship, totem- and image-worship. Even human sacrifice is said to lurk in the background behind the struggle of the faithful from dark age to the twilight. But where is the evidence? The fact that other peoples emerged from primitive animism, through polytheism to various degrees of approach to monotheism, does not prove that 'the line of faith' in the Old Testament did not preserve an original monotheism, which was specifically God-given. The evidence compels no such belief as that Israel's religious genius evolved the stubborn monotheism which is the Old Testament's most outstanding feature.

Criticisms of the 'religious' terminology and details of worship touch the Old Testament at another crucial point. The centre of Israel's worship was in the tabernacle (or 'tent' for worship) in which the sacred ark was kept during the wilderness wanderings and at Shiloh on arrival in the land of promise. Both the tabernacle and the later temple were associated with the ceremonial law, which provided for animal sacrifices. One cannot have it both ways. Either Israel was, in this respect, borrowing from the religious practices of the surrounding nations, or God did in fact direct that such sacrifices should be used in His worship. It is clearly necessary to choose. Either the

---

[1] Deism became a prevailing influence in the England of the eighteenth century. While believing in a general way that God originated the world, the deists accorded Him only a very general control of subsequent history.

reader will be inclined to regard the whole account and explanations of the Old Testament in this respect as an unnecessary, and somewhat repulsive, survival of the primitive tribal religious practices, or he will accept the Old Testament's explanation. It is to be noticed that this explanation pervades not only the rest of the Old Testament, but also the New. The explanation is that God expressly directed the use of such sacrifices as presenting a costly recognition by Israel of their faith in the coming Messiah, who would end all further sacrifice by His one complete sacrifice as the sin-bearer for the whole world. In the context of the Old Testament's account of Israel's holy God and of man's rebellion and sin, there is an appropriateness which is necessarily missed by all who decline to accept the Bible's own explanation of the religion of Israel.

Comment needs to be made concerning one further matter. In what is known as 'the Priestly Code' (Ex. xxv–xl, Leviticus and Numbers[1]) an outline is given of the ceremonial law of Israel. That it was expressly God-given is asserted, by implication in Ex. xxiv and directly in Ex. xxv. 1. A great deal of it is concerned with details which would be very appropriate all the while that Israel was in the wilderness, and yet would not be so appropriate in the land of promise to which they eventually came. Yet during this time, if the book were written towards the close of the wilderness wandering, Israel was eagerly awaiting a speedy entry into the land. These 'nomadic' features do not recur in the later Old Testament books. One reason, of course, may have been the attitude of the later prophets of Israel who were opposed, not indeed to the God-ordained ritual, but to Israel's wrong use of the temple ritual. 'This people worship me with their lips, but their heart is far from me,' was God's constant complaint, i.e. the ritual was never intended to be a substitute for, but rather a sign of, repentance and faith. Another reason is given in Heb. viii. 13: 'In that he saith, A new covenant, he hath made the first old. But that which is becoming old and waxeth aged is nigh unto vanishing away.' There is in the Bible a principle of development which is God-ordained. The progress of God's

[1] N.B.—In the 'Priestly Code', as viewed by most contemporary critics, Ex. xxxii–xxxiv and some sections of Numbers would not be included.

people is not simply one of haphazard growth or of human ingenuity. One is led to expect that on entering the land, or immediately prior to entry, the earlier and temporary Code will be superseded by a new Code, in which many of the wilderness details will be omitted or modified. This would appear to be the case in Nu. xxxv and xxxvi and in the book of Deuteronomy.

Some may object to the above that there is evidence that might suggest that it was the Priestly Code, and not the Deuteronomic Code, which was in force during the period of the second temple, i.e. from Ezra's time until the fall of Jerusalem. This might possibly be assumed from the regulations which were then in force for observing the Passover, whereas the Samaritans continued to keep this fast according to the Deuteronomic Code. It would not, however, follow from this fact that we must therefore necessarily conclude that the Priestly Code was written, or edited, at a late stage in Israel's history. As mentioned above, the impression made upon the reader's mind by some passages in the post-exilic prophets is that they regarded Israel as mistaken in the manner in which some parts of their worship technically was being carried out. The primary battle of the prophets was, of course, against idolatry, and especially against Baal-worship or its equivalents, yet they are also constantly concerned with Israel's glaring faults in carrying out the worship of the one true God. Whilst their appeals and warnings are directed mainly against Israel's idolatrous and rebellious state of heart, it is clear that the sacrificial offerings and the contemporary observance of the feasts were also technically at fault. The prophets appealed for greater spiritual maturity and purer worship. Israel, even in its ritual, cherished spiritual adolescence, and persisted in its partial obedience to the Law.

III. CRITICISM OF THE DOCUMENTS

It may seem to the reader that questions concerning the documents should have been put in the first place. This group of criticisms certainly looms the largest in the literature of the Old Testament. But literary analysis of the documents and the subsequent multifarious revisions and modifications of the theories arose when confidence in the history of the documents had already been weakened on other grounds. The allocation of an increasing number of sections of the earlier books of the Old Testament to writers of later periods arose from presuppositions such as that the religious teaching of the Pentateuch was too 'advanced' to have been written, as a whole, by Moses. To trace the many theories and their vicissitudes would require a very much bigger book than this can be. One of the most lucid accounts of the theories and their subsequent revisions will be found in *An Introduction to the Old Testament*, by E. J. Young. A brief sketch of the history of the speculations concerning the origin of the Pentateuch will be found in Appendix III (p. 136).

Here, it will assist clarity to confine attention to the three main lines of thought, which have been woven together into the more fully developed form of the 'Documentary Theory' of the Pentateuch. First, the hand of more than one author was suspected from the difference in the names which are given to God in different sections of the book. It was suggested that one writer worshipped God under the name 'Elohim' and the other under the name 'JHWH' (Jehovah, now usually transliterated Yahweh). The interest of those putting forward the theory was, of course, in the time at which the name Yahweh first began to be used in Israel. The documents came to be dated according to the views held on this matter. Second came the inferences which were made from the fact that the Old Testament does not appear to be interested in the Mosaic Law between Deuteronomy and later times when Josiah's reforms again brought it into a unique prominence. It was also claimed that the style and religious standards were too 'developed' easily to accord with a date which would place them in the period of the wilderness wanderings. Third, the ceremonial religious practices of Israel were thought to have developed through three main stages: (i) from earliest times until the reign of Josiah, when anyone could offer a sacrifice at any wayside shrine, and images of the deity similar to those of other nations were allowed; (ii) from Josiah's reign to the exile in Babylon, when there was a central temple in Jerusalem, and only priests (and Levites) were permitted to offer sacrifices on the altar; and (iii) the times subsequent to the return from exile, when the forms for full ceremonial worship were carefully codified and only the official priests could carry out the ritual required by the 'Priestly Code'. It was suggested in one of the later forms[1] of the Documentary Theory that the various parts of the Pentateuch corresponded to a writer 'JE' in the earliest period, 'D' in the second period, and 'P' in the last and fully developed period. Accordingly, the last writer in addition to his own contribution was regarded as the general 'redactor', or editor, who gave unity and final form to the whole.

If an ideal reader, entirely unbiased, could review the reasons which are given in the extensive writings on the problem of the Pentateuch for the popular theory which postulates three or four interwoven documents, surely certain very serious doubts must arise in his mind? Far too much seems to be based on too little evidence, and the predilections of the theorizers obviously play a very decided part in influencing their assertions. It has, for example, attracted the notice of the more conservative critics that Hegel's philosophy of history would seem to have played a greater part than linguistic, historical or archaeological fact in Wellhausen's theories concerning the Pentateuch. His philosophy, more than his scholarship, predisposed him to discount the historicity of the Bible's accounts of God's supernatural interventions on behalf of Israel. Again, it has been frequently pointed out how unsatisfactory is the method of dividing the Pentateuch on the basis of the names of God which are found in its various sections. Then, further, what are claimed to be duplications in the narratives ('doublets') on careful analysis and comparison of the texts are by no means proved to be so. Those who claim that comparable passages are necessarily 'doublets' also overlook the fact that repetition is necessary in any ordinary teaching method and that there is a place for repetition in securing due emphasis. Taken as a whole, it must remain extremely doubtful if such destructive analyses of the documents could ever have arisen apart from the prevailing

[1] The theory has had a number of variations. See Appendix III for a description of the final form of the Graf-Wellhausen Hypothesis.

philosophy of history and philosophy of religion in which they took their rise.

One important and interesting question has been recently raised by Dr. W. J. Martin. It concerns the meaning of a key sentence in the book of Exodus. Of the thirty or more reasons usually given in support of the Documentary Theory of the Pentateuch, all but two or three are of comparatively small importance. One, however, is clearly pivotal for the whole theory. In the Authorized Version of Ex. vi. 3, we read, 'And I appeared unto Abraham, unto Isaac, and unto Jacob, by the name of God Almighty, but by my name JEHOVAH was I not known to them.' The *not* is unexpected, and it appears foreign to the context of the preceding and subsequent verses. If the Authorized Version translation be correct, then the verse justifies the conclusion that the name 'Jehovah' (Yahweh) was not known to the Patriarchs, but came into use at some later time. God to the Patriarchs would thus be 'El', 'El Shaddai' or 'Elohim', but not 'Jehovah'. On the other hand, on what appears to be sound evidence, Dr. Martin challenges the understanding and translation of the verse in this way. He points out that in the Hebrew text the construction of the words which precede and follow the phrase 'was I not known' demands the expectation of a positive, not negative, statement. Citing five parallel constructions from elsewhere in the Old Testament, which are translated positively and presumably 'correctly', Dr. Martin claims that we have here an 'expletive interrogative'. If this were proved, then the translation would run somewhat as follows: 'I am the Lord (Yahweh); I suffered myself to be known unto Abraham, Isaac and Jacob by my name God Almighty (El Shaddai), *did I not* suffer myself to be known unto them by my name Lord (Yahweh)? I also established my covenant with them. . . .' Two further points support the suggestion that we have here an 'expletive interrogative' construction. The 'also' of the succeeding verse seems to follow more naturally and, in any case, since the covenant was with Abraham (confirmed to Isaac and Jacob), it would seem unlikely and incredible that the Patriarchs did not know the special covenant name of God. If Dr. Martin be proved correct, then one of the chief pillars, as originally stated, of the Documentary Theory will have been removed.[1]

It needs to be added that the above is only one example of weak links in the early theories concerning the structure and dating of the Pentateuch. Though it was very important at the close of the last century it has considerably less relevance to the current critical theories. It is simply cited here to show how slender were the foundations on which extensive structures have been erected in the earlier history of criticism. Today the average student will approach the problems of the Pentateuch by making a comparative study of the three bodies of legislation which are found in (i) Ex. xxi–xxiii; (ii) the 'Priestly Code' in Ex. xxv–xxxii and xxxiv–xl, Leviticus and most of Numbers; and (iii) Dt. xii–xxvi. He will then be encouraged to view, in the light of his findings, the various later problems connected with the sanctuary, the sacrifices, the priesthood, the various ceremonial feasts, the cities of refuge, the question of slavery, the regulations for the year of Jubilee and other matters which call for careful review and harmonization.

The scope of this book precludes adequate discussion of these. But the writer would observe that the grounds on which much of the theorizing has often been done are themselves wide open to criticism. Evolutionary theories concerning the development of religion in Israel are not valid grounds on which the authenticity of the documents of the Pentateuch can be questioned; the divine names as used in the Hebrew text do not provide valid data by which the documents may be divided and classified; there has been much too hasty assumption concerning the presence of repetitions or 'doublets'; and making comparisons between, and deductions from, the three Codes of law in the Pentateuch and the later books of the Old Testament (in the absence of adequate 'controls') is a very precarious process.

The Pentateuch is not the only part of the Old Testament which has received such treatment. The book of Isaiah, some of the Minor Prophets and, to some extent, the Psalms have attracted similar literary theories peculiar to themselves. It has

[1] In any case, the variation in the use of the divine names was always a precarious criterion for dating the MSS, and of little or no value later in the Pentateuch than Ex. vi.

mostly been with as little justification—especially that which differentiates by such uncertain criteria as those of style, and consigns some of the greatest prophetic passages to a period when there was general falling off in the quality of prophecy in Israel and when both the political stability and literary glories of Israel were at their lowest. It is after reviewing some of the minutiae of textual, linguistic, grammatical and historical evidence for the claims of the prevailing criticisms that the late Professor R. D. Wilson (Professor of Semitic Philology in Princeton Theological Seminary) can write: 'Nor, in spite of some apparent inconsistencies and of many passages difficult to explain satisfactorily, owing to an ignorance of all the facts, is there anything in the Old Testament that makes it appear incredible or unveracious. No one knows enough to affirm with confidence that any one of the prophetic books was not written by the man whose name it bears. No one knows enough to assert that the kings and others mentioned did not do and say what is ascribed to them' (*Is the Higher Criticism Scholarly?*, p. 58). His assertion has been made rather more, than less, true as a result of the further research which has been done since his death.

Professor W. F. Albright in *The Old Testament and Modern Study* (p. 25) emphasizes that upon this subject, as so many others, the evidence compels a new conservatism. He says: 'One theory is certain: the days when Duhm and his imitators could recklessly emend the Hebrew text of the poetic books of the Bible are gone for ever. . . . We may rest assured that the consonantal text of the Hebrew Bible, though not infallible, has been preserved with an accuracy perhaps unparalleled in any other Near-Eastern literature. . . . Incidentally, the mere fact that the translators misunderstood the meaning of innumerable words and phrases in Hebrew poetry so completely when putting the latter into Greek[1] in the second century B.C., should give us pause before suggesting that some of these poems had been composed in the very same century. No, the flood of light now being shed on biblical Hebrew poetry of all periods by Ugaritic literature guarantees the relative antiquity of its composition as well as the astonishing accuracy of its transmission.'

[1] i.e. in the LXX Version.

IV. CRITICISM FROM ARCHAEOLOGY

From the time that archaeology began to be scientifically studied (from about the year 1836, when Henry Rawlinson deciphered the Babylonian inscription on the rock face at Behistun, Iran) comparisons have been made with the history of the Old Testament. Two extreme tendencies were not long in making themselves felt. The one tended to claim that all archaeological finds were proving the accuracy of the biblical statements and the other pressed certain findings which at first appeared to conflict with the history of the Bible. In recent years more objective attitudes and more careful work has been done on both sides. Palestine itself, however, has been comparatively sparing of its yields, and, since most of the work has been more productive in Egypt, Iraq and other lands bordering on Palestine, the vast bulk of archaeological findings have had little direct bearing on Bible history. The chief biblical value of this science has so far been to emphasize the essential accuracy and intimate knowledge of local detail shown by the writers of the early books of the Bible. They are unlikely to have been composed as late as the first critics contended. The fair inference from the accurate background material of these books is that they were written at the time, or not long after, the events which they record.

In order that here we may not overstate the present position, let it be summarized by Professor H. H. Rowley in his 'Introduction' (p. xxi) to *The Old Testament Modern Study* (Edited H. H. Rowley): 'Exaggerated claims are sometimes made as to the significance of all the new archaeological material. It is suggested that it has proved the accuracy of Biblical records, or that it has conclusively settled such questions as the date of the Exodus. Such unfounded and misleading claims are dangerous. The evidence of archaeology is rarely as simple and clear as we would like to have it, and its bearing on Biblical questions is more often indirect than direct. Not seldom it complicates our problems rather than solves them. Nevertheless, it is true that in a broad way archaeology has tended to bring about a more conservative attitude to some questions. It has not proved the historical accuracy of the patriarchal narratives; but it has shown the historical credibility of those narratives by its evidence that they reflect the situation and the outlook of the patriarchal age in a remarkable way.' It might be added that anyone wishing to study how the outlook in archaeology has changed should read *Archaeology of Palestine*, W. F. Albright (Pelican, 1949).

In earlier years it was the practice of those defending the Bible to select the proper names of patriarchs and kings, the names of cities and other details given, and to show how archaeology had confirmed them. It is an endless task! Even if it were possible to check up on most or all of them, the knowledge would be of restricted value for the needs of our present study, except as showing the reliability of the details given in the books of the Old Testament. It is to be hoped, indeed, that much of the older types of criticism of the Old Testament have largely ceased. Archaeology has a way of producing the unexpected. For example, popular critics of the Bible in earlier times sought to make much of the fact that the Belshazzar of Daniel v was not referred to in secular history, that the final king of Babylon was Nabonidus, and that Darius the Mede is unknown to secular history, etc. But amongst later finds are those such as Cyrus' Annalistic Tablet (found in 1880) which provides us with the name of Belshazzar and his father Nabonidus, who was taken prisoner without resistance in Babylon. Other evidence indicates that Belshazzar held on for a longer period and was eventually surprised and killed in the part of the town which was situated on the opposite side of the river. Cyrus seems to have left Gobryas (who led the assault) to arrange for a governor to be appointed to the captured city. He was a Mede of royal descent. He appears to have appointed another Mede of royal descent, Darius, as governor, and the latter seems to have been allowed the title 'king', i.e. if we follow the account given in Daniel.

However, Professor E. J. Young (*The Prophecy of Daniel*, Eerdmans, 1949) has shown that all that is actually asserted in the text of Daniel is that, soon after Belshazzar had been slain, Darius the Mede took over the administration of the city of Babylon. It is not the case that a Median kingdom followed the Chaldean, for the Chaldean kingdom still remained as such.

Darius the Mede simply succeeded Belshazzar, who was a Chaldean, in the 'kingship' or governorship. Various attempts to identify Darius from secular history have been made. Some have thought he was Gobryas himself, but there is some evidence that the latter died a few days after the capture of the city. The fact is that there is no secular evidence available to place Darius in the background of the history of the day. The record given in Daniel is, of course, not proved nor disproved. But we have here an illustration of the way in which research has had a habit of throwing unexpected light (though not always satisfactory confirmation) on what earlier had been thought to be anomalies, anachronisms and inaccuracies in the Old Testament.[1] Archaeology has not yet identified Darius, but it does not follow that there was no such person and that Daniel was mistaken in his reference.

V. CRITICISM OF MIRACLES AND PROPHECY

A fifth group of criticisms are directed against the various instances of miracle and the claims to predictive prophecy which are recorded in the Old Testament. During the period when the prevailing philosophic outlook was dominated by the 'laws of uniformity' in nature and the illusion of the inevitability of human progress, records of supernatural interventions of God in history were an offence to the 'scientific mind'. Today there are powerful new tendencies in the world of thought, and the human mind is deeply divided. In some circles the prevailing outlook is more set against all idea of the supernatural and the miraculous. In others, it is more open to grant the possibility of miracle. Those influenced by the former group explain away 'the supernatural' to their own satisfaction by adducing coincidences in timing and a combination of circumstances from the ordinary scientific processes known to them. There are some minds which can accept everything which is 'miraculous' except what is re-

---

[1] Books for further study in which such evidence has been collected are: Millar Burrows: *What Mean these Stones?* 1941 (American Schools of Oriental Research); J. Finegan: *Light from the Ancient Past,* 1946 (Princeton University Press) and (more popular) S. L. Caiger: *The Bible and the Spade,* 1935 (O.U.P.); A. Rendle Short: *Modern Discovery and the Bible,* 1952 (I.V.F.) and *Archaeology Gives Evidence* (Tyndale Press).

corded as such in the Bible. The reason is not far to seek. The Bible can rarely be charged with advancing examples of miracle for miracle's sake. Its instances mostly have a clearly defined purpose and are bound up with the intervention of a personal God. Such an acknowledgment raises resistance in the thinking of modern 'autonomous' man.

a. Miracles

Instances of miracle pervade almost the whole of the Old Testament. It will not do simply to suggest that certain earlier superstitions have not been outgrown. There is no doubt, from the way in which the miracles are described, that they were believed by the writers to be the natural accompaniments of God's dealings with Israel. Several types of temporary suspension of the ordinary 'laws' of nature are described and the writers obviously expect that each instance of miracle will be accepted as such. The full list covers a wide range of human history, including the fact of the creation, the translation of Enoch and Elijah to heaven without death, the flood which covered the known world, the plagues of Egypt, Israel's crossing of the Red Sea, the gift of food to Israel in the form of manna and quails, the crossing of Jordan, the halting of the sun for half an hour for Joshua and its going backwards for ten degrees as a sign for Hezekiah, the miracles of Elijah's day, the deliverance from fire of the three heroic witnesses in Daniel iii, and of Daniel from the lions (Dn. vi. 15–23) and the saving of Jonah.

It is true that some of the Bible miracles may have had lesser parallels in later history which may to some extent be susceptible of scientific explanation. But the miracles recorded in the Bible are in the main *sui generis* and they are not open to ordinary scientific explanations. The crux of the matter is whether the reader is open to believe the revelation which God has given of Himself. There is nothing inherently improbable in any of the instances of God's interventions which are recorded, provided that God's being and character are accepted as described elsewhere in the Bible. This is not a matter which can be decided by scholarship. It is one which comes more in the sphere of the philosophy of religion, and the Bible's view of God.

b. Prophecy

Again, prophecy (in the form of prediction of the future) is often rejected on similar grounds. That is, it is not from any requirement of the linguistic[1] or textual study of the Old Testament, nor failure to find ample evidence that most of what was predicted in the Old Testament has been fulfilled, which influences the critic. It is rather an unwillingness to admit any explanation which requires a supernatural intervention and supersession of the ordinary human powers in transmitting the predictions. Most critics would, no doubt, grant that the seers of the Old Testament possessed 'enhanced insight' into the ways in which God works and so were able to make tolerably accurate forecasts of the likely future. But they refuse to go beyond this and they devote their attention to the exposition by the prophets of the 'burden' or message which they bore in relation to contemporary Israel. The essential point is that the grounds on which the average critic has rejected predictive prophecy has been not the 'scientific' findings, but *a priori* assumption that (beyond ordinary premonition and the accurate forecasts of a political genius) such 'supernatural' interventions as the Bible writers claim do not happen. The very critics who are apt to speak condescendingly of the 'naïve' faith, or 'obscurantism' of the conservative interpreter of the Bible, themselves give clear evidence of philosophic prejudice.

The Psalms and the prophetic books of the Old Testament are prolific in instances of pure prediction or prefiguration of future events. Even the Pentateuch has many key passages of this kind, for Moses was the greatest of the prophets until John the Baptist. Prophecy is intertwined in the warp and woof of many of the books. The supernatural is constantly breaking in. The fact that a considerable number of the books of the prophets consist of expositions, exhortations and warnings to the writer's contemporaries is not denied. But there are many passages in

[1] This remains true in spite of the work which has been done in elucidating the meaning of the Hebrew word *Na'bhi*, meaning 'seer' (or 'prophet'). Granted that much of some of the prophecies were 'preaching to the times', there are still a large number of predictions scattered throughout the Old Testament.

which the prophet's words are clearly predictive in a super-natural sense. For example, the prophet Isaiah's whole contention in the well-known passage concerning Cyrus (Is. xliv. 28 and xlv. 1) is that God had named in advance the conqueror who should eventually liberate Israel from Babylon and enable the temple to be rebuilt. As distinct from the idol-gods of the surrounding peoples, which 'know not, neither do they consider', the God of Israel was able in advance to name Cyrus His 'shepherd', who could fulfil His pleasure and unconsciously carry through all that God had determined for His people. God affirms: 'I have surnamed thee, though thou hast not known me' (Is. xlv. 4).

Similar examples of direct prediction are found elsewhere in Isaiah, for example, in Is. xxxvii. 26–36. When the mighty Sennacherib was threatening Jerusalem and all had given up hope of being able to offer any effective opposition, Isaiah calmly assured Hezekiah in God's name that 'He shall not come unto this city, nor shoot an arrow there. . . . By the way that he came, by the same shall he return . . .' (verses 33, 34). Later, in the event, 'the angel of the Lord' fell upon the camp of the Assyrians and they were driven back to Nineveh with great losses. On the other hand and on another occasion Micah, some hundred or more years previous to the event, asserts that 'Jerusalem shall become heaps' and that Judah shall go into captivity in Babylon; yet they should eventually be delivered (Mi. iii. 12, iv. 10). These and other similar predictions elsewhere in the Old Testament stand to be accepted or rejected not on grounds of linguistic, literary or scientific criticism but purely on the subjective grounds of the reader's views on the possibility or probability of supernatural and miraculous interventions by God in the affairs of men.

It should be added that the tendency at the present time amongst scholars is to allow for a greater degree of true prediction in the prophecies of the Old Testament. For example, in the writings of Professor H. H. Rowley will be found a number of passages which call the attention of the reader to the true elements of prediction which are present in the prophetic books. The present criterion which is laid down for dating such documents is that a given prophecy must be taken as earlier than what it predicts, though later than the background which it presupposes. As far as it goes, this is clearly a welcome gain in Old Testament study. However, the second half of the criterion does not necessarily follow, except where the writer himself clearly gives such historical or biographical background material. Some forms of prophecy, e.g. that which refers to events in the far distant future and messianic prophecy, is sometimes virtually independent of the background. Whilst it is true that much of what Israel's prophets wrote concerned the contemporary state of the nation and its immediate future, there still remains much that is pure prediction which is unrelated or only partially related to the contemporary scene.

IV. MORAL DIFFICULTIES

Since the present book is not intended to be a general treatise on Apologetics, a brief reference to the moral difficulties found in the Old Testament must suffice. A fuller discussion will be found in *Some Moral Difficulties of the Bible*, H. E. Guillebaud (I.V.F.), and also, in an older book sometimes obtainable second-hand, A. Saphir's *The Divine Unity of Scripture*.

It will be freely admitted by all honest readers of the Old Testament—even after every allowance has been made for progressive revelation and the slow stages of Israel's education—that there still remains a number of strange blots on the national and individual practice of what otherwise is the highest known official code of morals. The critics do not hesitate to point out the surprising and distressing instances of polygamy, slave-owning, personal immorality, imprecations and curses on one's enemies, blood-feuds and a cruel war of extermination in Canaan. It is not so much the repeated lapses of individuals or the nation which provide the most worrying feature. The real difficulty is that God Himself is described in the Old Testament contexts as commanding, or at least condoning, the questionable action in several of the instances which are cited.

Nothing is really gained by defending the Bible against such criticisms of the morality of its earlier books by (i) excusing the cruel acts of patriarchs or early Israel on the ground that they were common to the times and were to be expected at that stage; (ii) by pleading that the high code which was obligatory within Israel did not apply when they were dealing with Gentiles; or (iii) by suggesting—with some literary critics—that some of the writers were putting in the mouth of God what really arose from their own desire for revenge. The older commentators were on far sounder ground when they emphasized the fact that these various incidents were set in the context of a book which throughout emphasizes the general principles of God's moral government of the world. The lapses and cruelties of individuals show the desperately serious nature of human sin. Even the holiest fall below their own ideals, let alone those ideals which are God-given. The real answer to the moral difficulties lies in the Bible's own account of God's reactions generally to all forms of evil in the world. Evil is something which has mysteriously taken such deep root in man that not only must God judge it wherever it shows itself, but it is sometimes necessary for Him to work through a prevailing evil to bring about a new good. Activity in a situation which is beset by deep-seated evil may involve the one who intervenes in what seems to be acquiescence in it. This may often cause criticism of the reforming influence. For example, our Lord Himself was duly criticized for taking meals with hated tax-gatherers and 'sinners', i.e. with those who needed Him most.

In any case, it must be freely confessed that it ill behoves a generation which has so recently witnessed the depths of cruelty to which modern enlightened nations may sink in war-time to reflect unfavourably on Israel's morality. We must not allow critics of the Old Testament to forget the very high standard of the codes for worship and morals which Israel possessed. Whatever individual lapses there may have been, the ethical ideals of Israel had no equal—nor even a near competitor— amongst the ancient peoples.

CHAPTER NINE

DIFFICULTIES IN THE NEW TESTAMENT

THE books of the New Testament, as a whole, and especially the four Gospels, have had more scientific critical examination devoted to them than any other body of literature of the same size and antiquity. The scientific treatment of the Gospels, however, has not led to anything approaching so revolutionary a reconstruction as it has done in the case of the Pentateuch. This remains true in spite of the fact that better attested external historical data and far more background material for the period covered are available for such criticism. Ignoring the extreme and unreasonable attacks of those who in earlier Church history have opposed Christianity and, hence, have depreciated its 'title deeds', a reasonable application of modern scientific techniques to the New Testament is found to raise difficulties in only a few well-known problems.[1] These questions may be classified thus:

1. Can we accept the claims of the New Testament documents, viz. that they are contemporary, or first-century records of what they undertake to report?

2. How can we account for the similarities and the differences between the first three Gospels?

3. Was the fourth Gospel written at a later date than the first three, that is, at a time when Christian doctrine was more developed?

4. Can we accept as true the various accounts of miracles in the Gospels and the Acts of the Apostles?

5. How accurately informed was Paul concerning the life and teaching of Christ?

6. Should we accept as parts of the Canon the books of Hebrews, 2 Peter, 2 and 3 John and Jude?

[1] For a fuller consideration of these problems see *Are the New Testament Documents Reliable?*, F. F. Bruce (I.V.F.) and *Some Notes on the Gospels*, D. M. McIntyre (I.V.F.).

7. How can we account for the special character of the book of Revelation?

It is worth while to observe that, as in the case of the criticism of the Old Testament, the scholars who have examined the New Testament have tended to become more conservative. The problems are considerably less acute than they once were.

I. AN EARLY DATE FOR THE NEW TESTAMENT

In the late nineteenth century certain theories were put forward which had, as one result, the assertion that several of the books of the New Testament were written in the second century. It was, for example, suggested by the scholars of Tübingen (notably F. C. Baur) that a date not earlier than A.D. 130 or 140 for the Gospels, particularly the fourth Gospel, was required. The grounds, however, on which such late dates were put forward were not textual, historical, or archaeological, but largely philosophical. As in the case of Wellhausen's theories concerning the compilation of the Pentateuch, so here, Hegel's philosophy of history tended to divorce the contents of the documents from their historical setting and to necessitate conjectures based on their doctrinal contents which were thought to be too developed to be compatible with an early date. The New Testament critics virtually ignored both the evidence for earlier dating and the absence of evidence for late dating. The surprising fact might be noticed that historians and archaeologists (as, for example, Sir William Ramsay) have accepted the accuracy and also the early date of the New Testament, whilst the theologians for some years were more reluctant to do so.

The evidence for the New Testament is impressive. It may be fairly claimed that no other early MS has such a wealth of attestation. It is immensely greater than that for any of the classical authors. In addition to the two most important of the Greek Uncial MSS[1], there are nearly 3,000 Greek MSS of the whole, or part of, the New Testament. A number of these are earlier in date than the two Codices mentioned above, and some fragments go back to A.D. 175 or 200. In the Chester Beatty

[1] i.e. those written in the earliest style with capital letters and which were made about A.D. 350, e.g. Codex Sinaiticus and Codex Vaticanus.

Papyri (1931) are two Codices which contain almost all of the New Testament books and which were copied somewhere about A.D. 220–230. A third is thought to be from the late third century. In 1935 H. I. Bell and T. C. Skeat published fragments of MSS written on papyrus including 'Fragments of an Unknown Gospel' which, however, is now believed to be a paraphrase of the Gospel stories. These fragments appear to have been reliably dated not later than A.D. 150. Finally, a portion of a papyrus codex in the John Rylands Library, Manchester, was dated by Deissmann as existing from the time of the Emperor Hadrian (A.D. 117–138). It contains Jn. xviii. 31–33, and also verses 37 and 38. If the Papyrus MS was made where it was found in 1917, it reveals that John's Gospel had already reached Egypt by the reign of Hadrian.

Again, according to *The New Testament in the Apostolic Fathers* (Oxford 1905), the writings of the Apostolic Fathers (between A.D. 90 and 160) quote from a high proportion of the books of the New Testament. In the three earliest Christian books outside the Bible the 'Epistle of Barnabas' (between A.D. 70 and 80), the Didache (about A.D. 90), and 'the Epistle of Clement' (about A.D. 96) there are quotations from, at least, the first three Gospels, Acts, Romans, 1 Corinthians, Ephesians, Titus, Hebrews, 1 Peter, but also, possibly, from other books. This and other similar evidence more than justifies the comment by Sir Frederic Kenyon that 'both the authenticity and the general integrity of the books of the New Testament may be regarded as finally established' (see page 60 above).

II. THE SYNOPTIC PROBLEM

The difficulties which the differences in detail between the first three of the Gospels presented to scholars—commonly known as the 'Synoptic Problem'[1]—will be briefly considered in Appendix IV (p. 139). Here it will be sufficient to indicate that these Gospels contain a great deal of material which is identical in

[1] The Synoptic Problem is so named because it is concerned with the three, out of the four Gospels, whose material may be arranged in the form of a brief 'synopsis' of the life of our Lord, e.g. by placing it in three parallel columns, usually known as 'a Harmony of the Gospels'.

each, a considerable amount which is the same in only two of them and then, in addition, each Gospel has some material which is peculiar to itself. Bishop B. F. Westcott in his *Introduction to the Study of the Gospels* attempted to express these differences in percentages and on this basis (if we also include the Fourth Gospel in the comparison) the results are:

	Material peculiar to itself	Material in conformity with others
Mark	7	93
Matthew	42	58
Luke	59	41
John	92	8

Such a comparison at once raises several questions, of which the most important is: 'If Gospels are reporting on the same facts, how do they come to have so much which agrees with so much that differs?'

It is noteworthy that in the case of almost all the theories concerning the synoptic Gospels, insufficient attention seems to have been given to the contemporary setting and the virtual certainty that the writers possessed *direct* knowledge of the events and teaching which they were recording. They certainly pay too little attention to the Bible's claim to the Holy Spirit's function when aiding, inspiring and controlling the writers. Whatever scientific criticism may think about supernatural inspiration, at least the direct knowledge of the writer of the first Gospel (i.e. 'first' as it stands in our New Testament) must not be dismissed. If the first Gospel be written by Matthew, why should other 'sources' than his own sight and hearing be required? This disciple was closely associated with our Lord, almost for the whole period of His public life. He may, of course, have consulted others, e.g. concerning the early part of our Lord's life, but, on the other hand, he may also have been accorded by our Lord Himself a first-hand account of what he records. The same is markedly true in the case of John, the disciple whom the Lord admitted to special intimacy.

When, however, we come to Mark, Papias is quoted by Eusebius (*Eccl. Hist.* iii. 39) as saying that he 'neither heard the Lord nor accompanied Him.' Yet it is noteworthy that his home was Jerusalem (Acts xii. 12, 25) and that he had direct access to the apostle Peter. Luke's opportunity for direct contact with primary sources is not known, beyond the fact that he was the close companion of St. Paul. The apostle was a careful scholar. In addition, although he was called by special revelation to the apostleship after our Lord's ascension (Acts ix. 3–22; 1 Cor. xv. 3), he had had every opportunity to check his knowledge with that of the other apostles. Luke may, indeed, be referring primarily to the apostles in Lk. i. 1, 2.

The important fact needs to be noticed that, although we have been provided with 'portraits' of the Master from four different hands, the value and integrity of the four witnesses is emphasized by the fact that there are no obvious signs of collusion. The small differences may possibly find their explanation in the use by the writers of a variety of sources, both oral or written. Concerning the existence of an oral source, the words of Papias are not without relevance: 'But I shall not hesitate to put down for you along with my interpretations whatsoever things I have at any time learned carefully from the elders, and carefully remembered, guaranteeing their truth. . . . If, then, any one came, who had been a follower of the elders, I questioned him in regard to the words of the elders—what Andrew or what Peter said or what was said by Philip or by Thomas, or by James, or by John, or by Matthew, or by any other of the disciples of the Lord' (Eusebius *Eccl. Hist.* iii. 39). There is no need, however, to go outside the New Testament for evidence of an oral tradition for, in all probability, the essential teaching was unified during the time when the apostles were together for the forty days following the Ascension (Acts i. 1–14). Paul, also, appears to suggest that an oral tradition had been received from the Lord.[1] Some, however, of these references may need to be viewed as indicating that the knowledge had been received by special revelation. Yet in several instances there is a suggestion in the context that they were derived from an oral tradition. The available facilities of the writers for checking verbally their information would seem to have been more than adequate.

[1] Acts xi. 16; 1 Cor. vii. 10, ix. 14, xi. 23–25; 1 Thes. iv. 15.

Then, of course, there is the distinct probability that written sources existed. Some writers, for example Kirsopp Lake, suggest that Matthew 'almost certainly' quoted from a collection of 'proof-texts' compiled from the Old Testament.[1] Others think that Paul possessed a written memorandum of the teaching of Christ from which traces are found in his Epistles. For example, Acts xx. 35; 1 Thes. v. 2-5 and 1 Cor. xiii. 2; cf. Mt. xvii. 20, may indicate such quotations. But Luke gives the clearest indication that there were a number of other written records circulating and that he was especially anxious to ensure accuracy (Lk. i. 1, 2). For this purpose he went to those who were 'eyewitnesses and ministers'. Possibly this means that he had access to the other apostles, as well as Paul. Dean Alford concludes: 'That the Synoptic Gospels contain the substance of the apostles' testimony, collected principally from their oral teaching; that there is however no reason from their internal structure to believe, but every reason to disbelieve, that any one of the three evangelists had access to either of the other two Gospels in its present form.' Those who take this view claim that there is no clear *evidence*[2] which compels belief that Mark issued the first Gospel, and that Matthew and Luke used Mark and 'Q' (a lost written source or sources). On the other hand, there are careful, reverent and conservative scholars who are convinced by their study of the Gospels that there is sufficient evidence of direct relationship and dependence, e.g. of Mark upon Matthew or Matthew upon Mark, and of Luke upon Mark.

To return to the critics, some of the suggested difficulties seem purely subjective in their nature, depending on the viewpoint of the writer. At least it might be claimed that simple explanations and common-sense solutions are all that are necessary to harmonize some, at least, of the smaller divergencies in the four Gospels. For example, the four different versions of the official notice which was affixed to the cross of Christ are harmonized straightforwardly by the suggestion that the *full*

---

[1] Professor C. H. Dodd, however, in a recent study entitled *According to the Scriptures*, gives evidence for a different view (see page 71).

[2] See Appendix IV (page 139) for a review of the history of theories connected with the Synoptic problem.

superscription was: 'This is Jesus of Nazareth, the king of the Jews.' The fact is that because of the wide divergencies of view amongst themselves no satisfactory alternative has 'scientifically' been devised by the critics to take the place of the time-honoured view of the Church, namely, that in the synoptic Gospels we have three *independent* witnesses, who have been called upon by the Holy Spirit to put into writing the facts concerning the life and teaching of our Lord Jesus Christ. It would, indeed, be justly a matter for critical comment if the vast bulk of the three separate accounts did not agree. For, clearly, the writers would be likely to work mainly from the same 'material', would seek to derive their knowledge from the apostolic company or, where it was indirect, from the same alternative sources. The very fact, however, that the accounts are not identical repetitions adds to their value. It would seem that three truthful and accurate witnesses, without collusion, have given their accounts in a way which compels us to accept the validity of their message.

III. DATE OF THE FOURTH GOSPEL

Most modern writers regard the fourth Gospel as written at some considerable time after the others. The evidence, however, for its validity and early date is as great as that for any other New Testament book. It is quoted in some of the earlier writings of the Fathers. Ignatius, who was martyred about A.D. 115, seems clearly to quote from it. The Epistle of Barnabas is thought to echo Jn. i. 14, in the sentence, 'Because He was to be manifested in flesh, and to sojourn amongst us.' Numerous other early references have been recognized, and by the time of Irenaeus it is certain that he is to be found quoting from a book that had already taken its place in the Church.[1] As mentioned above, a papyrus containing five verses of Jn. xviii (which Kenyon asserts can be confidently assigned to the first half of the second century) was discovered amongst some papyri in the John Rylands Library, Manchester in 1920.

There is much in the fourth Gospel itself which supports the

[1] For the grounds on which some scholars assign the authorship of the fourth Gospel to John the Presbyter and a criticism of this position, see Appendix V (page 143).

conclusion that it was the apostle John who wrote the Gospel. Let us take three examples.

1. We have Peter's question, when the latter had thought that our Lord had meant to suggest that John 'the disciple whom Jesus loved' and 'who leaned on his breast at supper' was destined to live until His second coming. The incident is followed by the statement, 'This is the disciple which testifieth of these things, and wrote of these things; and we know that his witness is true.'

2. Obviously it was a Jew who wrote the Gospel, for the quotations from the Old Testament and his knowledge of the Jewish background is too intimate for it to be otherwise. It is also very clear from his accurate knowledge of the villages and details concerning Palestine that he was a Palestinian Jew.

3. The writer obviously was a contemporary of the events which he is describing; e.g. the writer is known to the High Priest (Jn. xviii. 15) and he knows Malchus (xviii. 10). He writes in i. 19–34 (particularly in verse 34: 'and I have seen and have borne witness that this is the Son of God') in a way which compels belief that he was a contemporary. There are many other incidental references in the book which confirm that it is very probable that John the apostle wrote this Gospel. It is interesting to compare Clement of Alexandria's comment that John wrote 'last of all' with that of Irenaeus: 'Afterwards, John, the disciple of the Lord, who also leaned upon His breast, did himself publish the Gospel during his residence at Ephesus in Asia.' Irenaeus also states that John lived until the time of Trajan (A.D. 98).

There seems no valid reason, then, for assigning the Gospel to any date later than A.D. 90–100, or to any writer other than the apostle John. No scientific evidence has been adduced for departing from the ancient tradition that the apostle wrote it in A.D. 96 after his release from exile by the Emperor Nerva. The grounds which some modern writers suggest for doing so, viz. 'the developed' nature of the doctrine and the difference from the synoptic Gospels, provide a very subjective and inadequate motive for discounting so much other strong internal and external evidence. Indeed, of John's Gospel it may be said, perhaps more than of any other book in the New Testament, that there is such a unity of aim and purpose, and also such a high spiritual tone, that some of the criticisms which have been made of this book are not only misplaced but even wanton. If some men did not stumble over and resist the plain message and contents of this book, many of the considerations which have been put forward would never have arisen. Here we have a touchstone for the whole of the Bible. It is a place where the would-be critic judges himself. The reader needs to accept or reject this book and its high claims as a whole.

IV. THE MIRACLES IN THE GOSPELS AND THE ACTS

In keeping with their attitude to the miracles in the Old Testament (see page 97) and to any explanation which involves an alteration in the ordinary course of nature, many modern thinkers are disposed to question the accounts of miracles performed by our Lord. It is, again, a question of evidence, of an understanding and interpretation of what actually is claimed in the text itself, and of one's general philosophical and scientific outlook. Already this matter has been discussed in relation to the Old Testament. Again it must be remarked that the real grounds on which the 'modern mind' dismisses the miracles recorded in the Gospels and the Acts is the last of these, i.e. the contemporary philosophic outlook. Hence, the real answer to those who would discount the message of the four Gospels on such grounds is the same as that which we must give for the New Testament as a whole. The essential question is: Does the reader of the Gospels accept the records of miracles, e.g. the changing of water into wine ('this beginning of his signs,' Jn. ii. 11), the feeding of the five thousand, the quelling of the storm on Lake Galilee, the many healing miracles, and the freedom from ordinary limitations of the resurrection body of our Lord? The central miracle is that of the resurrection of our Lord. The teaching of the rest of the New Testament turns on this pivotal event. If it is rejected, then the message of the Christian gospel is rejected. Such is clearly the contention of the apostle Paul in I Cor. xv. 1-19.

It is important to notice why the New Testament presents the evidence. As has been commented on pages 34, 35, the purpose of the miracles is to provide 'signs' to faith, and they occur mostly in a context which demands an affirmation of the divinity and saving power of Christ. In other words, the supernatural accompaniments of the revelation and of the saving gospel from God occasion no surprise in those who 'have faith in God' (Mk. xi. 22). The same happenings, however, are occasions of offence to those who are strangers to faith and to the power of God. It is worth while for a reader to reflect very seriously upon this whole matter. 'For if the dead are not raised, neither hath Christ been raised; and if Christ hath not been raised, your faith is vain; ye are yet in your sins. Then they also which are fallen asleep in Christ have perished. If in this life only we have hoped in Christ, we are of all men most pitiable' (1 Cor. xv. 16–19).

V. PAUL'S KNOWLEDGE OF CHRIST

Those who have difficulty in accepting Paul's authoritative interpretation and fuller explanation concerning the life, teaching and death of Christ, on the grounds that he had had no personal knowledge of Christ, underestimate the very distinct claims made by this apostle. To set up an artificial contrast between the teaching of our Lord as recorded in the Gospels and that of Paul in the Epistles does violence to the internal evidence. It is worth noting that Renan suggests that, putting together all the references to the words and deeds of our Lord contained in the Pauline Epistles, a writer would be well on the way to composing 'a small life of Jesus'. In fact nothing is clearer than that all of Paul's teaching, including that in which he might be considered to differ from the Gospel writers, is intended to be in harmony with the main apostolic tradition, and is in fact so. The difference is one rather similar to that which we find between the two forms of John's writing, i.e. between the direct account of Christ given in his Gospel and the interpretation and application of the facts provided in his Epistles.

The Old Testament knowledge of Paul—so far as its factual detail went—was probably superior to that of the other apostles (Acts xxii. 3 and Gal. i. 14). As for his knowledge of Christ, there is no doubt that he had excellent opportunities for gaining accurate information. After his conversion and his three years of awakening in Arabia and Damascus (no doubt a period in which, chiefly, the Old Testament became a new book to him) he 'went up to Jerusalem, to see Peter, and abode with him fifteen days.' Subsequently, he had contact with the apostle Peter, even rebuking him for his reluctance to admit the Gentiles, unless they would consent to be circumcised, into the full privileges of the Church (Gal. ii. 11). There is close agreement between the teaching of Paul and the doctrine of the rest of the New Testament, perhaps especially in the case of the Gospels. Also, we must not overlook that Paul claims a special revelation from God concerning those occurrences of which, as 'one born out of due time' (1 Cor. xv. 8), he had no opportunity to gain direct knowledge. He also claims revealed knowledge, e.g. in 2 Cor. xii. 1–12 and 1 Cor. ii. 10–16. So much so that he can add 'which things also we speak, not in words which man's wisdom teacheth, but which the Spirit teacheth. . . . We have the mind of Christ.' At the same time, he makes a special point of emphasizing that the gospel, which he preached, was precisely that of the other apostles (1 Cor. xv. 8–11, especially verse 11).

VI. THE VALIDITY OF HEBREWS, JAMES, 2 PETER, 2 AND 3 JOHN, AND JUDE

Of the books of the New Testament only a very few have had their validity seriously questioned. The chief reason for the doubt was certain omissions from the earliest lists of those books which were unanimously accepted by the early churches. A discussion of the details will be found in a treatise on the Canon of the New Testament.[1]

By the middle of the second century most of the New Testament was as we now have it. But Hebrews, James, 2 Peter, 2 and 3 John and Jude were not acknowledged by all, nor found in all contemporary lists of authentic books. Also, several books were included in these lists which were not eventually accepted by the churches as canonical; Eusebius (about 265–340) had doubts concerning only James, 2 Peter, 2 and 3 John, and Jude.

[1] For example, Alexander Souter *The Text and Canon of the New Testament* or B. F. Westcott *A General Survey of the History of the Canon of the New Testament*. See also page 103.

H

Both Athanasius (298–373) in the East and Jerome and Augustine in the West, give evidence in their specifications of 'Canonical' books which shows that by the year A.D. 400 all the books of our New Testament were accepted.

We must give due weight to the fact that the factor which more than any other contributed to such a small number of copies of Christian books being available from the first three centuries was probably the repeated persecutions when many MSS, in addition to persons, were destroyed. This is particularly true of the Edict of Diocletian (A.D. 303), requiring all Christian books to be destroyed by fire. The frequent persecutions, the rigours of travel and difficulties of copying the MSS, all added to the delay and difficulty of making an agreed collection of the authentic books of the New Testament. Chief of the difficulties which arose from such causes was the doubt whether—in the midst of the circulation of numerous pseudonymous and apocryphal books—James, Peter, John and Jude actually wrote the Epistles which bear their names. In the cases of Hebrews, 2 Peter and Jude, there was also hesitation concerning several passages in their contents which did not seem to be entirely homologous with the other parts of the New Testament.

The only book, however, on which any serious doubt has remained is 2 Peter. It was the latest book to receive any attestation. It does not seem clearly to have been mentioned in Christian documents until the time of Origen (about A.D. 230). It has been pointed out that there is strong resemblance to the Epistle of Jude and that it may depend upon this other book. Yet due regard must be accorded to the fact that the internal evidence is strong and that the writer claims to be Simon Peter; that there seems no reason for any other person's adopting the style 'Simon Peter' as a pseudonym in this case; and that there are—together with differences—a number of clear resemblances to 1 Peter, and it addresses the reader with the same apostolic 'tone'. The writer states that he had been with Jesus when He was transfigured (i. 16–18) and indicates that he expects early martyrdom as was foretold by our Lord for Peter (cf. 2 Pet. i. 14 and Jn. xxi. 18, 19). There are, however, some marked differences of style and a somewhat different vocabulary as compared with the first Epistle of Peter. In answer to this objection it has been pointed out that we know that Silvanus acted as scribe in the case of the first letter. There may have been another scribe or no amanuensis, in the case of the second. Others have emphasized certain references such as 'your apostles' (iii. 2), 'since the fathers fell asleep' (iii. 4), the controversy with Paul (iii. 15, 16), and a supposed reference to Gnosticism (chapter ii) as indicating a late date. It is a matter for which there exists insufficient data for a strong assertion to be made either way. It seems necessary to leave the matter as an open question. Even so careful and conservative an exegete as Calvin expressed a doubt. No other name than that of Peter, however, has been assigned by tradition to this letter, and it was accepted by the majority in the early Church.

VII. THE REVELATION

Difficulties have been expressed concerning the Johannine authorship and reliability of the Revelation. These have arisen because, first, the author simply names himself 'John' and does not give other signs of apostleship; second, it is the only example in the New Testament of so-called 'apocalyptic literature', apart from short passages such as Mt. xxiv; Mk. xiii; Lk. xxi; and 2 Thes. ii; third, the Greek of John's Gospel is considerably superior to that of the Revelation, in which there occur sometimes ungrammatical constructions and other defects; fourth, it is not until Athanasius that we have evidence that the book was accepted in the Eastern Church.

With regard to the second objection, the book is much in advance of other contemporary apocalyptic literature. The most important consideration, however, is that both internal evidence and external evidence are strong in support of the tradition which assigns the book to John the apostle. The four objections would seem to have been over-emphasized. The fact that the writer calls himself John (without adding the word 'apostle') loses its force when it is remembered that the first three chapters show that this letter went from Patmos to Ephesus in order to travel round the circuit of the seven churches where the apostle John had been ministering prior to his exile. The differences from the Gospel are small and, on balance, the similarities probably greater. There are also the characteristic Johannine emphases upon such phrases as 'the Word', 'he who overcomes', 'the slain lamb', 'the water of life', 'light' and 'darkness', 'life' and 'death'. The external evidence is as strong as for any other book of the New Testament, for traces are found in Barnabas, Ignatius, the Teaching of the Twelve Apostles. Both Justin Martyr and Irenaeus state that John wrote the book.

A more important practical question is how the modern mind can understand and interpret the unfamiliar imagery of such highly symbolical books as the Revelation. The key will be found, not so much in a study of the three or four main schools of interpretation, but in attention to the two following major considerations. First, the explanation of the imagery (or 'symbology') will be found in the Bible itself, e.g. in Ezekiel, Isaiah, Jeremiah, and the first Epistle of John. Second, the aim of the book of Revelation is not primarily to forecast history but to 'unveil' Christ. In Rev. i. 1, the literal meaning of the first phrase of the book itself is 'the unveiling of Jesus Christ'. It sets out to focus attention upon the ascended Lord, on the throne of God, powerfully warring against the Church's enemies, with the assurance that they will all be finally overcome.

CHAPTER TEN

THE INSPIRATION AND RELIABILITY OF THE BIBLE

WE have in the last three chapters briefly glanced at a few of the difficulties which confront modern educated readers when they come to the documents of Holy Scripture. It has been suggested that, whilst it is not true to say that the believing Christian need have no difficulties in considering the results of accurate linguistic, historical and scientific scholarship where they bear upon his Bible, yet these are really very minor in their nature. As explained in earlier chapters, they are almost all concerned with small details, and the majority of these are negligible. In certain cases there are found small defects in the transmission of the text, which mostly can be corrected, especially in the New Testament, from the large 'families' of MSS available. Even here such defects from copyist errors have not modified any basic Christian doctrine. Careful and distinguished scholars such as Westcott and Hort assert their conviction that the words of the New Testament about which there still need be any doubt are less than a thousandth part of the whole. It remains, however, to consider the Bible's own claims that the distinctive revelation given through the total personalities of the writers was supernaturally imparted and controlled by the Holy Spirit. In examining this claim it must be made clear that it is concerning the original (autograph) records of Holy Scripture that the claim is made.

What has been written in Chapter III under the paragraphs describing the 'Forms in which God spoke to men', and in Chapter IV, in the section in which are considered references to the older 'Holy Writings', need not be repeated here. But it may be well to refer again to some of the Bible's direct references to the inspiration and the reliability of the teaching of Scripture. The two ideas are not identical. The Bible's claim is that it is the divine inspiration which imparts the consequent reliability and authority to the record. The process of revelation may sometimes involve reporting on the deeds and words of wicked, as well as of good, men. Such references are included in the Scriptures for our due warning. At these points the authoritative record of God's revelation will bear a different connotation and lead to differing applications from, e.g., those of passages which bear the direct message of the gospel. But the idea of 'degrees' of inspiration is not a biblical one. Scripture emphasizes rather the differing *purposes* for which its inspired record has been given.

I. DIVINE INSPIRATION

Holy Scripture does not describe or define in any detail the process of inspiration. The fact is assumed in the same way that the existence of God is assumed throughout the books of the Bible. It, however, states emphatically the fact of its inspiration. Referring, presumably, to the Old Testament, Paul in 2 Tim. iii. 16, declares, 'All scripture is given by inspiration of God.' The form of the operative Greek word, as already indicated on page 46, is that of an adjective, i.e. 'All scripture is *theopneustic*,' i.e. 'is God-breathed' or 'breathed out by God.' A parallel thought is expressed in the Old Testament itself when the reluctant Jeremiah, after pleading his lack of intellect and of eloquence as a reason for being excused the uncomfortable duty of being a prophet, describes God's answer in the following words: 'Say not, I am a child: . . . whatsoever I shall command thee, thou shalt speak . . . the Lord put forth his hand, and touched my mouth, and the Lord said unto me, Behold, I have put my words in thy mouth' (Je. i. 7–9). Again, Peter, referring to the prophecies of the Old Testament, states: 'Knowing this first, that no prophecy of scripture is of private interpretation. For no prophecy ever came by the will of man: but men spake from God, being moved by the Holy Ghost' (2 Pet. i. 20, 21). The object of the reference is to emphasize that the message was given to them by God. The prophecy came (literally 'was brought') not by any human planning, but the writers were the 'mouth-pieces of God' and they were 'borne along by the Holy Spirit'. These are the only two outstanding references in Scripture itself to the form in which inspiration operated in the writers. On the other hand, the fact is acknowledged, or taken for granted throughout Scripture. It has been computed that writers in the Old Testament introduce their messages more than 3,800 times with 'The Lord spake,' 'the Lord said,' 'the word of the Lord came.'

The New Testament writers claim a comparable inspiration: Peter says that the 'commandment of the Lord and Saviour through your apostles' must be regarded as similar to 'the words which were spoken before by the holy prophets' (2 Pet. iii. 2). He puts Paul's Epistles on the same level as the Old Testament Scriptures (2 Pet. iii. 15, 16). Paul affirms that it is 'by word' or 'the commandment of the Lord' that he writes (1 Thes. iv. 15), though this may mean here that he is quoting a 'saying' of Jesus (cf. 1 Cor. xiv. 37). He also emphasizes that he is imparting the wisdom of God 'not in words which man's wisdom teacheth, but which the Spirit teacheth; comparing spiritual things with spiritual' (1 Cor. ii. 13). Calvin comments: 'If they were guided by the Spirit of truth when they published their writings, what prevented them from embracing a full knowledge of the gospel, and consigning it therein?'

As the Bible stands, it is clear that it presents itself as a homogeneous collection of sixty-six books, which were written on divine authority and which claim to have come through the human agents in such a way that the nature and accuracy of their contents would not be impaired. Of the process of inspiration, perhaps the best summary description has been offered in *Theopneustia*, by L. Gaussen, a former Professor of Systematic Theology in Geneva. He suggests the following statement: 'Inspiration is that inexplicable power which the divine Spirit put forth of old on the authors of Holy Scripture, in order to be their guidance even in the employment of the words they used, and to preserve them alike from all error and from all omission.' This definition neither exceeds nor falls short of the data which is presented by the Bible itself. The inference from Scripture itself is that the Bible is completely reliable for all the purposes for which God gave it (see 2 Tim. iii. 16, 17).

II. INSPIRATION AND MODERN OBJECTIONS

As has been suggested repeatedly in this book, the grounds on which the inspiration and reliability of the Bible have been

called in question are not in the last analysis linguistic, nor scientific. The ultimate grounds are the philosophical viewpoint and
presuppositions of the critics—whether it be a Hegelian philosophy of history or evolutionary materialism in one of its several
forms. Apart from minutiae such as a few defective numerals in
the Old Testament and what are called 'misquotations' of the
Old Testament in the New Testament (though these are often
partial quotations of familiar words or taken from the LXX
Greek version, rather than the Hebrew version) the major
problems presented by critics arise from their own viewpoints
and not from the Bible itself accepted in its true setting. Some
are unable to accept predictive prophecy, miracle and divine
inspiration as such, and so must therefore seek to account for the
inspiration of the Bible in other ways than what is stated in the
text of the Bible. The devotees of the 'scientific method',
wherever it is applied, tend to be agnostic, if not atheistic, in
their outlook. They are therefore open to our Lord's rebuke,
which is as true today as it has ever been: 'Ye do err, not knowing
the scriptures, nor the power of God.'

Until modern scepticism pervaded the modern educational
system, there was an almost complete unanimity in the Church
concerning the Bible. Professor L. Gaussen states: 'With the
single exception of Theodore of Mopsuestia' (whose writings
were condemned at the Council of Constantinople, 553) 'it has
been found impossible to produce, in the long course of the
eight first centuries of Christianity, a single doctor who has
disowned the plenary inspiration of the Scriptures, unless it be
in the bosom of the most violent heresies which have tormented
the Christian Church. . . .' There has, however, not been the
same unanimity since a veiled 'rationalism' under the guise of
'scientific method' pervaded the thinking of many Christians.
Those who appear convinced that they have, to their own satisfaction at least, achieved a synthesis between a rationalistic
'scientific' method and Christian faith, tend to show clearly the
effects of an all-pervading humanism. Their view of God and
the world remains essentially 'deistic' and their view of the Bible
suffers accordingly. With a lower view of the Bible comes a
lowered view of the divine activity in daily life. There is a very

close practical association between a true acceptance of the Bible (as the Christian's valid and dependable rule of faith and conduct) and his ethical attainment. It is of no small practical importance in the life of the Church that its title deeds should be recognized as valid and its source of guidance as fully reliable. The question therefore arises, 'As we review the place of the Bible against the background of the modern world, can we still regard it as the accurate and completely reliable record of God's revelation to man?' Whilst L. Gaussen may have been able to stress the consistent testimony to the plenary inspiration of the Scriptures throughout the eight first centuries of Christianity, can this older belief in the Bible still be maintained in the light of all the advance in modern knowledge?

III. PLENARY INSPIRATION

It is the conviction of the writer that an unequivocal doctrine of the 'plenary inspiration' of the Scriptures can, and must, be maintained by the Christian today. If a reader would prefer to substitute 'verbal inspiration' for the words 'plenary inspiration'—so long as he allows the due and proper place which Scripture itself accords to the personalities of the human writers —then, in the view of the writer, he would be equally correct. The grounds on which he may do so are derived from the Bible's whole concept of the character of God and of the methods which He uses; from the nature and internal claims of the Scriptures themselves and especially of the New Testament; and from the absence of any significant findings of modern science which contradict an accurate exegesis of the relevant passages of Scripture. There is not space to argue the point, but it might well be asked how God would ordinarily be expected to give an all-important revelation or message to men (such that it could truly be called 'inspired' and 'reliable') and yet for it to be inaccurate to affirm that the *words* are controlled. It would be a case of an inspired message given in uninspired words. Nor is it true to the claims of Scripture to assert in the manner of some of the current theories that 'the writers themselves were inspired, but the products of their writing were not necessarily inspired.' Let us again hear Paul on this point: 'which things also we speak, *not in words which man's wisdom teacheth, but which the Spirit teacheth*' (1 Cor. ii. 13).

It is a matter of common observation that the same preacher or theological lecturer who, out of the pulpit, carefully fences his words when speaking of inspiration and is somewhat scornful of those who adhere to the Bible's own view of its nature, is compelled to act as if he accepts the plenary inspiration of the words as soon as he wishes to preach with any authority. The moment that he turns from 'an essay in the pulpit' and really takes to evangelical preaching, from that moment he is compelled to treat the words of the Bible as the very Word of God. The apostles—particularly Paul and Peter—imply as much almost in so many words—as, for example, in the Corinthian and Pastoral Epistles. A preacher of the last century, F. D. Maurice, gives his view in the following words: 'When you speak to me of verbal inspiration, though I do not like the phrase . . . I yet subscribe most unequivocally to the meaning which I suppose is latent in it. I have no notion of inspired thoughts which do not find for themselves a suitable clothing in words. I can scarcely, even in my mind, separate the language of a writer from his meaning. And I certainly find this difficulty greater in studying the Bible than in studying any other book; the peculiarities of its language seem to be strangely significant.'

IV. 'INFALLIBILITY'

The word 'infallible' as applied to the Bible has in late years become unpopular or 'lowered' in meaning. Some would even suggest that it is an illegitimate term. But it is to be noted that it is taken directly from the Latin *infallibilitas*, which is the exact equivalent of the Greek *asphaleia* as used by Luke in his preface to the Gospel.[1] The passage might be translated: 'it seemed good to me also, having had perfect understanding of all things from the very first, to write unto thee in order, most excellent Theophilus, that thou mightest know the *infallibility* of those things wherein thou hast been instructed.' The Greek *asphaleia* is derived from *a* (a negative prefix) and *sphallo*, 'to trip up,' the noun *asphaleia*

---

[1] This fact should give pause to those who are so fond of remarking that 'the word infallibility is not a scriptural word'.

meaning 'certainty', 'safety' (cf. its use in Acts v. 23; 1 Thes. v. 3, and Acts xxi. 34, xxii. 30; cf. Heb. vi. 19, 'an anchor of the soul, a hope both *sure* and *stedfast*'). When used in this way and as meaning 'that which does not lead astray', but which is 'sure and steadfast', we would contend that it is not only scriptural, but it is wholly true, to describe the Holy Scriptures as 'infallible'.

V. DISCREPANCIES IN REPORTING THE SAME FACTS

In making the above statements the author has not overlooked small discrepancies of detail in the Old Testament—e.g. that Jehoiachin, in 2 Ki. xxiv. 8, was said to have been eighteen years old at his accession, whereas in 2 Ch. xxxvi. 9, he is said to have been eight; or that in Gn. xxxii. 3, Esau is said to have been in the land of Seir (Edom) when Jacob returned into Canaan, whereas in Gn. xxxvi. 6–8, Esau is said to have gone to Seir after Jacob had occupied more than his fair share of the ancestral land. There are similar minutiae in the historical books and other small discrepancies elsewhere in the text as we now have it.

Between the accounts of similar incidents in the Gospels there are found minor discrepancies. For example, in the report of the healing of the centurion's servant in Mt. viii. 5–13, we appear to be told that the centurion came himself to Jesus, whereas in Luke vii. 1–10, it would seem that two groups of intermediaries were sent. The difficulty, however, is in the English translation of Matthew's account, where the Greek word employed is equivalent to the use in modern English of the phrase to 'approach' someone. This may often be through intermediaries. Again, in Mt. viii. 28, it is said that there were two Gadarene demoniacs healed, whereas the Mark and Luke accounts cite only one. But the text shows that our Lord remained with the man who had been freed from the legion of demons, and there was ample time for another to come from the same district to be healed. It is noteworthy that it was Matthew, and not Mark or Luke, who was the eyewitness. Finally, the most important of the discrepancies is, of course, that found in the latter parts of the two genealogies of our Lord. There is not necessarily, however, a contradiction here. Those who regard Mary as also being of Davidic descent would point out that Matthew, writing from Joseph's point of view, traces the lineage of Joseph, whereas Luke, writing from the point of view of the Mother of our Lord, traces Mary's descent. A more probable explanation, however, is given by the late Prof. J. Gresham Machen in *The Virgin Birth of Christ*, where he adduces good reasons for regarding both genealogies as being those of Joseph. The one in Matthew presents the official royal lineage of the Messiah, and kingship sometimes was transmitted (as in modern times) through cousins, whereas Luke's account provides us strictly with the actual human descent. It is noteworthy that Matthew goes back only to Abraham, whereas Luke is concerned to go back to Adam.

The majority of these small discrepancies and residual problems are clearly due to defects in transmission and to similar explicable causes. Yet, even so, and after full consideration of the fact that the MSS at the disposal of scholars today are in this way slightly defective, the writer would maintain that we are still justified in claiming a 'virtual', 'essential' infallibility for the 'resultant text' of Holy Scripture. Certainly the internal evidence encourages us to claim that the autograph copies of the divinely inspired Scriptures were infallible as originally given.

VI. THE AUTHORITY OF HOLY SCRIPTURE

The view of the authority of the Bible which has been put forward in this book is refused by some modern theological writers on the grounds that there exists—as they think—at its heart a dualism. The writings of the Evangelical Protestant Reformers, and particularly those of Calvin, have in late years been subjected to criticism from this point of view. It is contended, for example, that the Reformer's statements concerning the validity and intrinsic authority possessed by the Bible are offset by the accompanying doctrine of 'the inner witness of the Holy Spirit.' In effect, the critics suggest, there are presented two sources of authority. But such an objection is based on a radical misunderstanding. If Calvin be carefully studied, as for example in his *Institutes* Book I, vii and viii, there is neither ambiguity nor contradiction concerning this matter. This writer is quite unequivocal in his claim that final authority resides in

Holy Scripture solely because it is inspired by God. We are to accept the rule of Scripture over our thoughts because God is its Primary Author. This fact alone gives the Bible its objective authority, and nothing must be allowed to dispute its claim.

The authority of Scripture is not derived from the fact that there is 'the inner witness of the Holy Spirit' which accompanies this Word and confirms it to our minds and hearts. The function of this witness of the Spirit is to 'persuade' the believing man to accept the authority which is already antecedently in Scripture, and to apply this authoritative Word to his daily living. This witness is something which is corroborative and which persuades and convinces us of the authority which it derives only from its divine origin.

A similar misunderstanding tends to attach itself to the Evangelical view of 'the inner witness of the Holy Spirit', in relation to 'saving faith' in the gospel. It must be strongly insisted that it is not the case that the Bible becomes in itself an object of 'saving faith'. The function of the witness of the Spirit to Scripture is to bring the would-be Christian man to a deep confidence in the Bible *generally*, i.e. to accept God's revelation as a whole. Such a confidence in Scripture is necessary in preparation for any effective appreciation of the Person, work and words of Christ. For where else is there any true picture of Christ or valid formulation of His teaching? It is from the matrix of a *general* certitude that Holy Scripture is God's authoritative *word* to man that there is born that *special* confiding faith which finds rest only in its particular and satisfying Object—Jesus Christ, the only Mediator between God and Man.

The words of the first chapter of the Westminster Confession of Faith continue to provide one of the most accurate and satisfying statements concerning the Bible: 'The authority of the Holy Scripture, for which it ought to be believed and obeyed, dependeth not upon the testimony of any man or church, but wholly upon God (who is truth itself), the author thereof; and therefore it is to be received, because it is the word of God.'

'We may be moved and induced by the testimony of the Church to an high and reverend esteem of the Holy Scripture, and the heavenliness of the matter, the efficacy of the doctrine, the majesty of the style, the consent of all the parts, the scope of the whole (which is to give all glory to God), the full discovery it makes of the only way of man's salvation, the many other incomparable excellencies, and the entire perfection thereof, are arguments whereby it doth abundantly evidence itself to be the word of God; yet, notwithstanding, our full persuasion and assurance of the infallible truth, and divine authority thereof, is from the inward work of the Holy Spirit, bearing witness by and with the word in our hearts.'

'All things in Scripture are not alike plain in themselves, nor alike clear unto all; yet those things which are necessary to be known, believed and observed, for salvation, are so clearly propounded and opened in some place of Scripture or other, that not only the learned, but the unlearned, in a due use of the ordinary means, may attain unto a sufficient understanding of them.'

'The infallible rule of interpretation of Scripture is the Scripture itself; and therefore, when there is a question about the true and full sense of any scripture (which is not manifold but one), it must be searched and known by other places that speak more clearly' (*Westminster Confession of Faith*. Chapter I, Sections iv, v, vii and ix).

CHAPTER ELEVEN

UNDERSTANDING THE BIBLE

Arose may be studied in several ways. It may be cut from
the tree and placed in a vase. It may be described as a
whole and painted. Its petals can be removed one by
one and its more intricate structures more closely examined.
Its main structures can also be sectioned, stained and inspected
under the microscope. Or, for those who choose this way, it
may be dried, pressed and set up as a museum-piece. In just the
same way, one could rear a small eaglet in a zoological garden
until the full-grown and sorry-looking eagle strives to achieve
room to stretch its wings in flight. Or, this powerful bird can
be killed, stuffed and set up in a glass case. Or, again, it can be
dissected until its feathers and skeleton are all that remain. But
when everything has been said, the place at which to feast on
the beauty and fragrance of a rose is in a rose garden. The eagle
is a fascinating bird. Yet no true impression of its full speed or
skill is possible until one has climbed near to its eyrie on some
frowning crag. From there alone can one really observe it,
cleaving the air to strike down its prey.

The Bible, ordinarily, does not yield up its treasures to the
careless reader. It must be accepted on its own terms. For its
interpretation extraneous knowledge which has been drawn
from far and wide is not the first consideration. It desires to be
its own interpreter. It asks that 'spiritual things' shall be compared with 'spiritual'. They must not be forced into some strange
humanistic or scientific mould. It is at its best only when seen
against its own background.[1] It is the Word of God addressed to
sinful and rebellious mankind through Christ the only Redeemer

[1] The most effective way to appropriate for oneself the inner message
of the Bible is to make time for a short daily reading of, say, one chapter.
The majority of students and busy workers find this possible, and to the
fullest extent rewarding, only if they can keep an undisturbed half an
hour before breakfast, or late in the evening. Or, for some, it must be a

and true Revealer. Its world of philosophy is that of Christ. From Him we receive the true view of God, of His temporal creation and of mankind, of sin, of Christ's saving work and new creation. Its history is 'the history of salvation.'[1] In the first place it traces the initiative and intervention of God in choosing, leading and saving the nation of Israel in Old Testament times in order that it might provide the matrix from which at length might come the divine Redeemer. Its pivotal point is the death and resurrection of Christ. To this all leads forward in the Old Testament and from this all succeeds and comes to full completion in the New Testament. Its supreme aim is to portray the glory of God revealed in history by the disciplining and saving of sinful man. Hence, from the ascension of Christ, the New Testament history is concerned chiefly with the new Israel, the Church of which Jesus Christ is the Lord and Head. The fact of His Headship alone accounts for its saving vitality, and, indeed, for its survival. The Church, to use a phrase borrowed by John Wesley from an old Puritan writer, is 'the life of God in the souls of men'.

It is, then, above all else necessary to place oneself in a spirit of humility before the Book and to let it speak to us. We must allow it to address us in its own language and its own forms of illustration.[2] We must recognize from the outset that much of what our humanistic education has taught us concerning the meaning of the world and of human nature is not necessarily a

weekly and more leisurely event. Such Christians use this time by commencing with a short prayer that they may understand the spiritual significance of what they are about to read. After the reading they reflect carefully upon what they have read. They then conclude with prayer that these things may be worked out in their own personal lives and in the communities in which they live and work. See the booklet *The Quiet Time*, edited by Bishop Frank Houghton (I.V.F. 9d.).

[1] German theology uses the word 'Heilsgeschichte' to emphasize the central purpose of the historical facts recorded in the Bible.

[2] Perhaps some will feel that more should here be said concerning the understanding of detailed and difficult points. But these will largely take care of themselves if the central issue of right attitude and main theme be grasped. For an introduction to the interpretation of the Bible and for an explanation of its use of parable, allegory and figurative language, see *Understanding God's Word* by the Rev. Alan M. Stibbs (I.V.F., 2s. 6d.)

true view. The accent of the Bible throughout falls upon God's complete and unassailable sovereignty over the world and the beings which He has made. It declares Him to be implacably hostile to human sin and rebellion. It records His just judgments on both nations and persons. Only then and in this context does it begin to provide a gleam of hope and to open up the new way through Christ into His holy presence. Even here access is only possible for the truly humble and penitent sinner who comes in faith and obedience. The New Testament offers the gift of God, i.e. 'eternal life', only in this setting of the unique work of Jesus Christ as the Sinbearer and Substitute. His resurrection alone brings 'life and immortality to light through the Gospel.' Indeed, this is the centre in actual human experience. For unless a man grasps the message of the Bible at this point, its deepest meaning will remain closed to him. A change is demanded in his whole outlook and nature.

Our Lord goes so far as to insist that this change must be so radical as to amount to a 'new birth'. Such a change can be effected only by the Holy Spirit, the inspirer and interpreter of the Bible. For this purpose God has promised to impart His Spirit to the earnest seeker. In the words of our Lord: 'If ye then, being evil, know how to give good gifts unto your children, how much more shall your heavenly Father give the Holy Spirit to them that ask him?' (Lk. xi. 13). Our Lord Himself provides in a conversation with Nicodemus, a ruler of the Jews, the most direct teaching which we have in the Bible concerning the importance of this matter:

'Except a man be born anew, he cannot see the kingdom of God. Nicodemus saith unto him, How can a man be born when he is old? can he enter a second time into his mother's womb, and be born? Jesus answered, Verily, verily, I say unto thee, Except a man be born of water and the Spirit, he cannot enter into the kingdom of God. That which is born of the flesh is flesh; and that which is born of the Spirit is spirit. Marvel not that I said unto thee, Ye must be born anew. The wind bloweth where it listeth, and thou hearest the voice thereof, but knowest not whence it cometh, and whither it goeth: so is every one that is born of the Spirit' (Jn. iii. 3-8).

I

The essential source of enlightenment and interpretation of Holy Scripture is the Holy Spirit. In returning to the question of the final authority which must control and guide the Church or the individual Christian it is again necessary to emphasize with the Protestant Reformers that we must keep firmly in mind that it is the Holy Spirit, accompanying Holy Scripture, who corroborates it as the guiding light. The important fact is that the Spirit is He through whom the Word was written. Yet, as Calvin has commented, Christ rules the Church through the *sceptre* of His Word. The loyal and enlightened subject will treasure the sceptre for what it is and devote himself to obedience even when he cannot always understand. Our obedience is not to some soulless decree or abstract philosophy. Our Lord declared truly: 'The words that I have spoken unto you are spirit, and are life' (Jn. vi. 63).

Finally, to the one who diligently seeks there will at length come the deepest insight that can be afforded to the spiritual man. One of the most moving descriptions of how it comes are found in the words of Charles Simeon, an eighteenth-century Fellow of King's College, Cambridge:

'It was but the third day after my arrival (i.e. as a freshman) that I understood I should be expected in the space of about three weeks to attend the Lord's Supper. "What?" said I, "*Must* I attend?" On being informed that I must, the thought rushed into my mind that Satan himself was as fit to attend as I; and that if I must attend, I must *prepare* for my attendance there. Without a moment's loss of time, I bought the *Whole Duty of Man*, the only religious book that I had ever heard of, and began to read it with great diligence; at the same time calling my ways to remembrance, and crying to God for mercy; and so earnest was I in these exercises that within the three weeks I made myself quite ill with reading, fasting and prayer.

'The first book I got to instruct me in reference to the Lord's Supper (for I knew that on Easter Sunday I must receive it again) was Kettlewell on the Sacrament; but I remember that it required of me more than I could bear, and therefore I procured Bishop Wilson on the Lord's Supper, which seemed to be more moderate in its requirements. . . .

'My distress of mind continued for about three months, and well might it have continued for years, since my sins were more in number than the hairs of my head; but God in infinite condescension began at last to smile upon me, and to give me a hope of acceptance with Him.

'But in Passion Week, as I was reading Bishop Wilson on the Lord's Supper, I met with an expression to this effect: "That the Jews knew what they did, when they transferred their sin to the head of their offering." The thought came into my mind, What, may I transfer all my guilt to another? Has God provided an Offering for me, that I may lay my sins on His head? Then, God willing, I will not bear them on my own soul one moment longer. Accordingly I sought to lay my sins upon the sacred head of Jesus; and on the Wednesday began to have a hope of mercy; on the Thursday that hope increased; and on the Friday and Saturday it became more strong; and on the Sunday morning, Easter-day April 4, I awoke early with those words upon my heart and lips, "Jesus Christ is risen today! Hallelujah! Hallelujah!" From that hour peace flowed in rich abundance into my soul; and at the Lord's Table in our Chapel I had the sweetest access to God through my blessed Saviour.'

O.T. Ref.	Matthew	Mark	Luke	John	To Whom Addressed
Gn. i. 27, v. 2, ii. 24	xix. 4, 5	x. 6-8			Pharisees
Ex. iii. 6	xxii. 32	xii. 26	xx. 37		Sadducees
Ex. xx. 12 Dt. v. 16 Ex. xxi. 17	xv. 4	vii. 10			Scribes and Pharisees
Ex. xx. 12-16 Dt. v. 16-20 Lv. xix. 18	xix. 18, 19	x. 19	xviii. 20		Rich young ruler
Dt. vi. 4, 5	xxii. 37	xii. 29, 30	x. 27		One of the Pharisees, Lawyer, one of th Scribes
Lv. xix. 18	xxii. 39	xii. 31	x. 27		One of the Pharisees, Lawyer, one of th Scribes
Dt. vi. 13 Dt. vi. 16 Dt. viii. 3 Dt. xix. 15 Dt. xix. 15	iv. 10 iv. 7 iv. 4 xviii. 16		iv. 8 iv. 12 iv. 4	viii. 17	Satan ,, ,, Disciples The People
Ps. viii. 2 Ps. xxii. 1 Ps. xxxi. 5 Ps. xxxv. 19 or lxix. 4	xxi. 16 xxvii. 46	xv. 34	xxiii. 46	xv. 25	Chief Priests and Scribes A prayer to God ,, ,, ,, ,, Disciples
Ps. xli. 9 Ps. lxxxii. 6 Ps. cx. 1	xxii. 44	xii. 36	xx. 42, 43	xiii. 18 x. 34	Disciples The Jews Pharisees
Ps. cxviii. 22	xxi. 42	xii. 10, 11	xx. 17		High Priests and Scribes
Is. vi. 9, 10 Is. xxix. 13 Is. liii. 12	xiii. 14, 15 xv. 8, 9	iv. 12 vii. 6, 7 xv. 28	viii. 10 xxii. 37		Disciples Pharisees and Scribes Disciples
Is. liv. 13				vi. 45	The Multitude
Is. lvi. 7 Je. vii. 11 Is. lxi. 1, 2 Ho. vi. 6	xxi. 13 ix. 13	xi. 17	xix. 46 iv. 18, 19, 21		Those in the temple Those in the synagogue Pharisees
Ho. vi. 6 Zc. xiii. 7 Mal. iii. 1	xii. 7 xxvi. 31 xi. 10	xiv. 27 i. 2	vii. 27		Pharisees Disciples The Multitude

REFERENCES TO THE OLD TESTAMENT

R.T.S. 1925. Quotations are taken from the Authorized Version)

Occasion	Introductory Words
Question concerning divorce	'Have ye not read?'; He 'said'; 'What therefore God hath joined.'
Question concerning resurrection	'Have ye not read?'; 'Spoken to you by God'; 'God spake'; 'Moses . . . calleth.'
Complaint of unwashen hands	'God commanded.' 'Moses said.'
Question about eternal life	'Thou knowest the commandments,' 'Keep the commandments.'
The first commandment	'The first of all the commandments is.'
The first commandment	'The second is like unto it.'
Third temptation	'It is written.'
Second ,,	,, ,, ,,
First ,,	,, ,, ,,
Discourse on forgiveness	
The Light of the World	'It is written in your law.'
Children's hosanna	'Have ye never read?'
On the cross	,, ,, ,, ,,
,, ,, ,,	,, ,, ,, ,,
Last discourse	'That the word might be fulfilled that is written in their law.'
Last supper	'That the scripture may be fulfilled.'
Discourse on 'Ye are gods'	'Is it not written in your law?'
Discourse against Pharisees	'How then doth David in spirit call him Lord?' 'David himself said by the Holy Ghost.' 'David himself saith in the book of Psalms.'
The Stone rejected	'Did ye never read in the scriptures?' 'What is this than that is written?'
Parable of the sower	'In them is fulfilled the prophecy of Esaias.'
The washing of cups and pots	'Esaias prophesied of you . . . , as it is written.'
Last supper	'This that is written must yet be accomplished in me.'
Bread from heaven	'It is written in the prophets.'
Cleansing of the temple	'It is written'; 'Is it not written?'
Teaching in Nazareth	'This day is this scripture fulfilled in your ears.'
Call of Matthew	'Go ye and learn what that meaneth.'
Plucking of the corn	'If ye had known what this meaneth.'
Before betrayal	'It is written.'
John's messengers	'This is he of whom it is written.'

BIBLIOGRAPHY

Any reader who may wish to study further some of the main suggestions of the foregoing chapters is referred to the following short bibliography. It is mainly confined to those books written from a theologically conservative viewpoint.

I. THE VOICE OF GOD IN THE CHURCH

Calvin, John: *Institutes of the Christian Religion* (Book I: vi and vii).

Davies, R. E.: *The Problem of Authority in the Continental Reformers.*

II. THE BIBLE IN ITS PRESENT SETTING

Lamont, Daniel: *Christ and the World of Thought.*

Machen, J. Gresham: *The Christian Faith in the Modern World.*

III. GOD'S SELF-REVELATION

Orr, J.: *Revelation and Inspiration.*

Warfield, B. B.: *The Inspiration and Authority of the Bible.*

IV. THE FIRST DOCUMENTS

Stonehouse, N. B., and Wooley, P.: *The Infallible Word.*

V. THE COMPLETION OF THE DOCUMENTS

Bruce, F. F.: *The Books and the Parchments.*

Kenyon, Sir Frederic G.: *Our Bible and the Ancient Manuscripts.*

VI. OUR LORD'S BIBLE

Manley, G. T.: *It is Written.*

Machen, J. Gresham: *The Origin of St. Paul's Religion.*

VII. DIFFICULTIES FROM SCHOLARSHIP AND THE SCIENCES

Kenyon, Sir Frederic G.: *The Bible and Modern Scholarship.*

Wilson, R. D.: *Is The Higher Criticism Scholarly?* or *A Scientific Investigation of the Old Testament.*

Kenyon, Sir Frederic G.: *The Bible and Archaeology.*

Short, A. Rendle: *Modern Discovery and the Bible.*

Short, A. Rendle: *Archaeology Gives Evidence.*

The American Scientific Affiliation: *Modern Discovery and the Christian Faith.*

Standen, Anthony: *Science is a Sacred Cow.*

VIII. DIFFICULTIES IN THE OLD TESTAMENT

Aalders, G. Ch.: *A Short Introduction to the Pentateuch.*

Orr, J.: *The Problem of the Old Testament.*

Young, E. J.: *An Introduction to the Old Testament.*

Young, E. J.: *My Servants the Prophets.*

Young, E. J.: *The Prophecy of Daniel.*

Guillebaud, H. E.: *Some Moral Difficulties of the Bible.*

Saphir, A.: *The Divine Unity of Scripture.*

IX. DIFFICULTIES IN THE NEW TESTAMENT

Bruce, F. F.: *Are the New Testament Documents Reliable?*

McIntyre, D. M.: *Some Notes on the Gospels.*

Thiessen, H. C.: *An Introduction to the New Testament.*

X. THE INSPIRATION AND RELIABILITY OF THE BIBLE

Stonehouse, N. B., and Wooley, P.: *The Infallible Word.*

Warfield, B. B.: *The Inspiration and Authority of the Bible.*

XI. UNDERSTANDING THE BIBLE

Atkinson, B. F. C.: *The Christian's Use of the Old Testament.*

Houghton, F.: *The Quiet Time.*

Manley, G. T.: *The New Bible Handbook.*

Stibbs, A. M.: *Understanding God's Word.*

Tasker, R. V. G.: *The Old Testament in the New Testament.*

A BRIEF HISTORY OF THE DOCUMENTARY THEORY
OF THE PENTATEUCH

(Summarized from pp. 120–153 of *An Introduction to the
Old Testament*, by E. J. Young)

I. THE EARLIER DOCUMENTARY HYPOTHESIS

There had been various forms of embryonic criticism from
earliest times, e.g. the disparagement of the Old Testament by
Marcion (A.D. 138) and also the attacks of Celsus. The first
considerable theory to emerge in modern times was that by
Jean Astruc in his book on Genesis, 1753. He suggested that
though Moses may have been responsible for the Pentateuch as we
have it, yet he 'must' have incorporated earlier documents written
by patriarchs concerning events which happened 1,000 years or
more previously. The chief 'clues' were the use of the divine names,
e.g. Elohim and Jehovah. Astruc's work applied chiefly to Genesis.

II. THE FRAGMENTARY HYPOTHESIS

Later a somewhat different view was taken by Alexander Geddes
(1792), Johann Vater (1805), A. T. Hartmann (1831) and, to
some extent, W. M. L. De Wette (1806). They suggested that
the Pentateuch was unified as a whole at a period of history later
than that of Moses. The final editor of the Pentateuch was thought
to have worked on a series of fragments from earlier records.

III. THE CRYSTALLIZATION HYPOTHESIS

Henrich Ewald (1845), August Knobel (1861), and Eberhard
Schraeder (1869) indicate what they believe to be the most
ancient passages, which they think were afterwards embedded
in books by later writers and editors. For example, Moses is
accepted as the author of the Ten Commandments and of some
of the other laws. The simplest form of this hypothesis was based
on the conviction that there were two original documents—
the First Elohist and the Second Elohist (the latter being more

theocratic), which were worked over and unified by the 'Jehovist' writer. Deuteronomy was said to be the work of another writer.

IV. THE DEVELOPMENT HYPOTHESIS (GRAF–WELLHAUSEN)

A more detailed and developed hypothesis was eventually submitted to Old Testament scholars as a result of the work of J. W. Colenso (1879), Karl H. Graf (1866), Abraham Kuenen (1870), and Julius Wellhausen (1877). Wellhausen's form of the hypothesis postulates that the early part of the Pentateuch has come from two documents—the Elohist and the Jehovist, the latter combining them into one narrative. Deuteronomy was added later and integrated with the rest in the time of Josiah. The whole of the Pentateuch was then revised, and also Joshua. The 'priestly legislation' (in the Elohim Document) was largely the work of Ezra and the passage from the seventeenth to the twenty-sixth chapter of Leviticus was said to date from the time of Ezekiel. It was this Graf-Kuenen-Wellhausen hypothesis which chiefly influenced Old Testament studies in this country in the late nineteenth and early twentieth century.

V. FORM–CRITICISM

Hermann Gunkel in 1901 came forward with the suggestion that Genesis consisted of the oral traditions; i.e. various early tales, 'sagas', and 'myths' were handed down verbally until they were all recorded. Though originally fragmentary, the various stories 'crystallized' around some 'hero' such as Abraham or Jacob. At a later time the documents were collected into groups —J or E— and eventually unified. Hugo Gressmann analysed Exodus on similar lines. (It is important to note that much of the work of this school essentially undermines the Graf-Kuenen-Wellhausen theory.)

VI. THE NEW DOCUMENT HYPOTHESIS

Walter Eichrodt (1916) proposed two Jehovist writers, and in 1922 Otto Eissfeldt suggests the L (or J) is the 'laity' or secular source and suggests L, J, E, and P as the four constituents of the Pentateuch.

VII. DEUTERONOMY

Between 1914 and 1929 new work was done on Deuteronomy. The earlier 'certainty' that Deuteronomy was the product of Josiah's reign was challenged. Johannes Hempel (1914) allotted editorship to a priest at the time of the centralization of worship. These documents were thought also to incorporate other ancient traditions and sources. A. C. Welch contended for a considerably earlier date for Deuteronomy.

VIII. MODERN DEVELOPMENTS

A number of modifications in these theories have been introduced in recent times. One recent writer (Professor E. Robertson) tends to bring the date of most of the Pentateuch forward to the time of Samuel. Other modifications, suggesting an even earlier date for the completion of the books, have been considered by competent scholars. It is not possible at this stage to forecast what is likely to be the next phase of Pentateuchal criticism.

IX. COMMENTS

Throughout the history of the various forms of the Documentary Theory, there have been a number of well-informed opponents. The very conflicts and vicissitudes through which the theory has passed indicate the insecure grounds on which it is based. Considerable harm has been done because generations of theological students have not been made more aware of the actual position and how few grounds there have been for the impression that there was 'proof' for the prevailing attitude of distrust of Old Testament history.

A BRIEF HISTORY OF THEORIES CONCERNING THE SYNOPTIC PROBLEM

(Summarized from *An Introduction to the New Testament* by H. C. Thiessen)

I. EARLY PERIODS

From earliest times various endeavours have been made to harmonize the Gospels, e.g., the 'Diatessaron' of Tatian. Such attempts continued through the Middle Ages until Lachmann first fully discussed the problem as we know it.

II. THE UREVANGELIUM (PRIMITIVE SOURCE) THEORY

G. E. Lessing and J. G. Eichhorn proposed that there was an earlier source, or original Gospel, from which the three Synoptic writers drew their materials. It was also suggested that during the time when those Gospels were being produced this source was itself going through revisions. There seems to be little historical or literary support for this view.

III. THE INTERDEPENDENCE THEORY

Grotius suggested that one of the writers first produced his Gospel, the next used his Gospel, and the third the two predecessors. There was, however, considerable disagreement concerning which Gospel appeared first.

IV. THE FRAGMENTARY THEORY

Schleiermacher put forward the view that the main sources were neither an oral tradition nor written Gospel, but that a series of short narratives were edited and revised and written over. This theory has the merit that it might claim to accord with Lk. i. 1, 2.

V. THE ORAL TRADITION THEORY

Westcott, Ebrard, Alford, Godet and others asserted that the original common basis for the Gospels was entirely oral and derives from the period of the apostles' stay in Jerusalem (Acts i. 1–viii. 4). There is no doubt a good deal of truth in this view, but it does not go far enough. It would account only for the parts which are common to all three of the Gospels.

VI. THE TWO-DOCUMENT THEORY

Eichhorn, B. Weiss and Holtzmann propose that there were two sources. The first was like, or probably actually was, the Gospel of Mark. The second (now commonly called 'Q' from the German word 'Quelle', meaning source) provides the material which is not contained in the second Gospel, but which is common to Matthew and Luke. Many believe that this second source was the collection of sayings (Logia) of our Lord, which are referred to by Papias. The tendency today is to accept Mark's Gospel (and not a hypothetical 'Ur-Markus', i.e. the original Mark) as the first source and to regard 'Q' as a collection of 'sayings of our Lord'.

VII. THE FOUR-DOCUMENT THEORY

Whilst some German critics have postulated three sources, in Britain the more popular tendency has been to conclude that there were four. Canon B. H. Streeter, who at first had advocated a Two-Document hypothesis, in his later writings, e.g. *The Four Gospels* (1925), puts forward the Four-Document theory. This has proved the most widely held view in recent years so far as Britain is concerned. It is really an elaboration of the Two-Document theory and may be represented roughly as follows. Mark is regarded as the first of the three Gospels to be written, and Matthew and Luke are believed to have had this Gospel before them and to have used it with some degree of freedom. Matthew is regarded as using (i) Mark's Gospel, (ii) 'Q', i.e. the material which is common to Matthew and Luke, (iii) 'M'—a Matthean source, used only by Matthew, and (iv) an oral source (the Antiochene tradition). Since Luke does not adhere to Mark so closely as Matthew, Streeter suggests that Luke prefers, rather than Mark's Gospel, to use some other alternative source. He therefore proposes a source 'L' (i.e. reflecting the material not

found in Mark or Matthew), a large section of which (ix. 57–
xviii. 14) is known as 'P', because it provides an extensive
account of our Lord's ministry in Peraea. Streeter suggests that
'Q' and 'L' together formed a first edition of Luke's Gospel, i.e.
'Proto-Luke'. It is further suggested that the account of the
infancy of our Lord and the material from Mark was later added
to 'Proto-Luke' in order to give us the present form of Luke's
Gospel.

VIII. ORAL SOURCES AND THE 'FORMGESCHICHTE' SCHOOL

Martin Dibelius in 1919 suggested that the Gospels should be
studied from the point of view of the 'literary forms' which are
contained in the Gospels as we have them. These literary forms
were thought to correspond to the various oral traditions which
were circulating when the documents were written. According
to this view there are six 'forms' for the stories which the Gospels
preserve: (i) the passion; (ii) stories of Jesus' deeds which support
the message; (iii) stories of healing, etc.; (iv) legends and edifying
narratives of saintly men; (v) sayings or speeches of our Lord;
(vi) interpretations of the stories and sayings.

There is room for much difference of opinion on such an
analysis and those using this approach differ considerably
amongst themselves. Professor Albright comments: 'Only
modern scholars who lack both historical method and perspective
can spin such a web of speculation as that with which form-
critics have surrounded the Gospel tradition. The sureness with
which early Christian leaders distinguish between the normative
and aberrant sayings of Jesus becomes very clear when we analyse
the so-called 'agrapha' or apocryphal 'logia' collected from
extant and from recently excavated documents. The 'agrapha'
generally express gnostic or antinomian ideas which are foreign
to the Gospels.' . . . 'From the standpoint of the objective
historian, data cannot be disproved by criticism of the accidental
literary framework in which they occur, unless there are solid
independent reasons for rejecting the historicity of an appreciable
number of other data found in the same framework.'

IX. A CONSERVATIVE ESTIMATE OF THE FACTS

The reader who gives first place to the Bible's own statements concerning such problems will note certain features in the evidence. The writers (except for one or two passages in the prophetic books) are not described in such a way as to suggest that they had no need of careful attention to verifiable facts, i.e. they were not writing in a mechanical fashion. In the case of the Gospels it may be that (i) the writers used 'sources'; at least, we know that one writer (Luke) used them for purposes of comparison (Lk. i. 1–4). (ii) They may have used, at least on some occasions, material derived from the apostles. In the case of Matthew, the writer was no doubt most influenced by his own first-hand acquaintance with the teaching and work of Christ. At times, they may also have used an oral tradition or earlier accounts written during our Lord's lifetime. (iii) Writing under the influence of the Holy Spirit, they could claim our Lord's own promise of a heightened accuracy of memory and whatever is intended by the words 'I have yet many things to say unto you, but ye cannot bear them now. Howbeit when he, the Spirit of truth, is come, he shall guide you into all the truth.' Cf. 'The Comforter, even the Holy Spirit . . . shall teach you all things, and bring to your remembrance all that I said unto you' (Jn. xvi. 12, 13 and xiv. 26).

There seems to be no conclusive reason why we should not regard the Gospel writers as three accurate and truthful witnesses who have been called upon by the Holy Spirit to give their separate accounts of the same facts. They would have had an essentially similar background for their personal experience and their knowledge was derived from the same group of persons, or sources. On the other hand, those who believe that a comparison of Matthew, Mark and Luke (particularly in the Greek text) reveals signs of the dependence of Matthew and Luke upon Mark may be allowed their view which does not diminish the value nor the authority of the synoptic Gospels. For a more detailed study of this problem see *Are the New Testament Documents Reliable?* F. F. Bruce (I.V.F.). Compare also *Some Notes on the Gospels*, D. M. McIntyre (I.V.F.).

THE AUTHORSHIP OF THE FOURTH GOSPEL

Those who dispute the fourth Gospel's apostolic authorship and assign it to John the Presbyter seem to do so on very inadequate grounds. Their case rests mainly upon the reference by Papias (as quoted in the *Hist. Eccles.* of Eusebius). Eusebius, who died about the year 340, quotes from Papias for whom a date early in the second century, possibly 115–130, is accepted. After mentioning that he had endeavoured to ascertain all possible facts concerning the Lord's deeds and teaching from the 'Elders', and those who were acquainted with the 'Elders', he enumerates the latter as Andrew, Peter, Philip, Thomas, James, John, Matthew. He asserts his interest in what they 'said', and then continues 'or by any other of the disciples of the Lord, and what things Aristion and the Presbyter John, the disciple of the Lord, *say*'. Eusebius comments upon this, noting the interval between the mention of the two Johns, 'the other John he mentions after an interval, and places him among the others outside of the number of the apostles, putting Aristion before him, and he distinctly calls him a presbyter. This shows that the statement of those is true who say that there were two persons in Asia that have the same name, and that there were two tombs in Ephesus, each of which, even to the present day, is called John's.'

To conclude, however, from the statement of either Papias or Eusebius that a separate person—John the Presbyter, and not John the apostle—wrote the Gospel is a questionable procedure. First, Eusebius does not seem too sure of his facts concerning the two Johns. Second, all the apostles in the earlier list are called both 'presbyters' and 'disciples', and so in the second instance there is no necessary denial of John's apostleship in the phrase 'the Presbyter John, the disciple of the Lord'. If the same person, the apostle John, wrote both Gospel and the Epistles, then it is noteworthy that in 2 and 3 John the writer calls himself 'the Elder', rather than 'apostle'. This, again, is in keeping with what we might anticipate from his customary understatement. There is every bit as much justification for inferring that, in contrast with the impression made on Eusebius, Aristion and the Elder (who was also the apostle) John were still living. The strength of this inference is increased when we note that there is a change from the past tense 'said' in the first list, to the present tense 'say' in the case of the last two names. This is much strengthened by his addition—'For I do not think that what was gotten from the books would benefit me as much as what came from the living and abiding voice.' Why then should we not conclude that John, Elder and Apostle, (together with Aristion, who had known Christ) was still living when Papias wrote?

Some scholars have put forward theories of either multiple authorship, or various stages of composition. But, with the possible exception of the section Jn. vii. 53–viii. 11, a strong impression is made on the reader that this book is a coherent and unified whole. As Professor Sanday has remarked: 'The one rock on which it seems to me that any partition theory must be wrecked is the deep-seated unity of structure and composition which is characteristic of the Gospel'. Others have criticized the divergence in form of this Gospel and its presentation of Christ, as compared with those of the Synoptic writers. But the writer has specially emphasized that the aim of the book is not to provide a biography, but a statement which will have the effect of causing people to believe in Christ. If one carefully reads the fourth Gospel in the light of the others, there is obviously no difference between its presentation of Christ and that of the other Gospels. All alike clearly present the same Lord Jesus Christ. The purpose of this Gospel cannot be sufficiently emphasized: 'Many other signs therefore did Jesus in the presence of the disciples, which are not written in this book: but these are written, that ye may believe that Jesus is the Christ, the Son of God; and that believing ye may have life in his name' (Jn. xx. 30, 31).